"In this collection of spiritual sayings, now in its first English translation, Armand-Jean de Rancé reflects on spirituality as lived faith that realizes relationship with God through the obliteration of one's own will and self-love. The *Pensées* are brief and practical, yet deeply thoughtful. David N. Bell provides a thorough and engaging context for the spiritual background and contributions of the *Pensées*. It is fitting that Rancé, who would have once seemed an unlikely author of spiritual edification, and whose *Pensées* made their way through the world in several haphazard editions, now finds a home in a series dedicated to a variety of spiritual thought."

— R. Jacob McDonie, Associate Professor of Literatures and Cultural Studies, University of Texas-Rio Grande Valley

"David Bell provides a fresh presentation of Rancé with his excellent new translation of the 'Thoughts and Reflections' of the French reformer. A substantial introduction provides a clear context for what follows, and the reflections themselves are remarkably contemporary. They are powerfully succinct and rich in insight. This work presents the wisdom of Armand-Jean de Rancé as absolutely relevant and significant for our own time. I am grateful for this superb book and hope it will attract a wide audience, especially among those in my own Order."

— Sister Maria Rafael, OCSO, Tautra Mariakloster, Norway

CISTERCIAN STUDIES SERIES:
NUMBER TWO HUNDRED NINETY-SEVEN

Armand-Jean de Rancé and Jacques Marsollier

Thoughts and Reflections of Armand-Jean de Rancé, Abbot of la Trappe

Introduced and translated by
David N. Bell

α

Cistercian Publications
www.cistercianpublications.org

LITURGICAL PRESS
Collegeville, Minnesota
www.litpress.org

A Cistercian Publications title published by Liturgical Press

Cistercian Publications
Editorial Offices
161 Grosvenor Street
Athens, Ohio 45701
www.cistercianpublications.org

Biblical quotations are translated by David N. Bell.

1   2   3   4   5   6   7   8   9

Library of Congress Cataloging-in-Publication Data

Names: Rancé, Armand Jean Le Bouthillier de, 1626–1700, author. | Marsollier, Jacques, 1647–1724, author. | Bell, David N., 1943– translator.
Title: Thoughts and reflections of Armand-Jean de Rancé, Abbot of La Trappe / Armand-Jean de Rancé, Jacques Marsollier, David N. Bell.
Other titles: Pensées et réflexions. English
Description: Collegeville, Minnesota : Cistercian Publications, Liturgical Press, 2022. | Series: Cistercian studies; two hundred ninety-seven | Includes bibliographical references and index. | Summary: "In 1703, three years after Armand-Jean de Rancé's death, Jacques Marsollier, one of Rancé's biographers, published a volume of selected Pensées et Réflexions, "Thoughts and Reflections," by Rancé. They are 259 of the essential ideas of the prolific writer and abbot presented in a condensed form"— Provided by publisher.
Identifiers: LCCN 2022002927 (print) | LCCN 2022002928 (ebook) | ISBN 9780879071349 (paperback) | ISBN 9780879071363 (epub) | ISBN 9780879071363 (pdf)
Subjects: LCSH: Rancé, Armand Jean Le Bouthillier de, 1626–1700. | Trappists—France. | BISAC: RELIGION / Monasticism | RELIGION / Christianity / Catholic
Classification: LCC BX4705.R3 A25 2022 (print) | LCC BX4705.R3 (ebook) | DDC 271/.125—dc23/eng/20220525
LC record available at https://lccn.loc.gov/2022002927
LC ebook record available at https://lccn.loc.gov/2022002928

Contents

Part Two
The Translation

Abbreviations

CS   Cistercian Studies series. Cistercian Publications.

SBOp   Sancti Bernardi Opera. Editiones Cistercienses.

SC   Bernard of Clairvaux. Sermones de Cantica Canti-
corum.

Preface

This book offers the reader an English translation of Armand-Jean de Rancé's Thoughts and Reflections, *Pensées et Réflexions*, selected by Jacques Marsollier, archdeacon of Uzèz, and published for the first time in 1703, three years after Rancé's death. Marsollier himself died in 1724. I first came across the book some years ago in a catalogue of *Livres anciens et modernes* put out by the bookseller Picard in Paris. Since I have a liking for seventeenth- and eighteenth-century books in their original bindings and original condition—it is one of my lesser sins—and since I also have a liking for the writings of the abbot of la Trappe, I paid the bookseller 180 euros and, in due course, received a charming duodecimo in a contemporary binding of the *Pensées et réflexions de M. de Rancé, Abbé de la Trappe*, published by Chez Vente in Paris in 1767. This, as we shall see in chapter two, is the third edition of the *Pensées*. The volume also contains a paraphrase of the seven penitential psalms. I should add that this was some time before the book was digitized by Google and made freely available on the World Wide Web as an ebook.

Since I was occupied with other things at the time, I put the book on the shelf and, to be quite honest, forgot about it. Much more recently I came across it again, spent an hour reading the *Pensées*, and realized that what Marsollier was trying to do was to bring Rancé out of the cloister, penetrate to the heart of his spirituality, and make him accessible to a wider audience. When, finally, I had read all the *Pensées*, I was sufficiently impressed to make an English translation in the hope—perhaps,

I admit, vain—that English-speaking readers, especially Cistercians of the Strict Observance, might be tempted to dip into it and find therein a rather more impressive spirituality than they had expected.

Rancé himself tends to be verbose in his writings—he is far from being alone in this: it was a verbose age—and, generally speaking, he and his contemporaries would never write one page when ten would do. The *Pensées* are all short, and although I cannot say that they are easily digestible, each of them takes but a few seconds to read. They will take much longer than that to ponder, but most people will be more tempted to read the three brief *Pensées* on (for example) humility and humiliations than the almost one hundred pages on the same subject of Chapter XII of Rancé's *De la sainteté et des devoirs de la vie monastique*. "It is with words as with sunbeams," said the nineteenth-century poet laureate Robert Southey, "The more they are condensed, the deeper they burn."

DNB

Part One

Introduction

Chapter One

Armand-Jean de Rancé, Abbot of la Trappe

Armand-Jean le Bouthillier de Rancé was born in Paris on 9 January 1626.[1] He was one of a number of surviving children, with one elder brother, one younger brother, and five sisters. The family was well to do and enjoyed close relationships with important figures both at the royal court and in the ecclesiastical hierarchy. Armand-Jean de Plessis, Cardinal Richelieu, was the young Rancé's godfather, and Rancé was named Armand-Jean in honor of the illustrious cardinal. His elder brother, Denis-François, had never been robust, and when he died, not unexpectedly, in 1637 at the age of seventeen, Armand-Jean found himself facing a career not in the military (as his family had first envisaged), but in the church. In other words, he was taking over where his deceased brother had left off. Since Denis-François had possessed a number of valuable benefices before he died, these now came to Armand-Jean, and at the age of eleven he found himself prior or commendatory abbot

---

[1] What follows is essentially a summary (with some additions) of the material in David N. Bell, *Understanding Rancé: The Spirituality of the Abbot of La Trappe in Context*, CS 205 (Kalamazoo, MI: Cistercian Publications, 2005), xv–xxv. For a much more detailed account, see Alban J. Krailsheimer, *Armand-Jean de Rancé, Abbot of la Trappe: His Influence in the Cloister and the World* (Oxford: Oxford University Press, 1974).

3

of five religious houses, one of them being the dilapidated Cistercian abbey of la Trappe in the wilds of Normandy.

A commendatory abbot, we might add, was an abbot who was appointed by the pope or local ruler, not elected by his own community. The abbots so appointed were normally secular prelates who were given the abbeys as rewards for services rendered, and, for the most part, they were no more than absentee landlords whose main concern was to pocket as much of the monastic revenues as they could. In this they succeeded splendidly; with but a few exceptions, the commendatory system was an unmitigated disaster for French monasticism.[2]

The young Rancé was educated at home by tutors until it was time for him to enter the Collège d'Harcourt of the University of Paris. That he was an intelligent and dedicated student is not in doubt, and he actually published his first book at the age of thirteen. This was a commentary on the Greek poet Anacreon; it was introduced by a dedicatory letter, also in Greek, to his godfather Cardinal Richelieu.[3]

Rancé took his MA in 1646 and then began to make his way in society. Two years later he was ordained as a deacon by Paul de Gondi, the future Cardinal de Retz, and in 1651 as a priest by his uncle, the archbishop of Tours. By this time he was the head of his family, his father having died in 1650, and one of the properties he had inherited was a country estate at Véretz,[4] just about two hundred kilometres (as a French bird would fly) southwest of Paris. He loved the place and spent as much time there as possible. By 1654 he was a doctor of theology of the Sorbonne, and a year later his uncle sent him as a delegate to the General Assembly of the Clergy of France. Once there, he did all that was required of him, but found the proceedings

---

[2] See further Bell, *Understanding Rancé*, 53–55.

[3] See Bell, *Understanding Rancé*, 253–55.

[4] See Louis A. Bossebœuf, *Le Château de Véretz: son histoire et ses souvenirs* (Tours: Imprimerie Tourangelle, 1903).

too long, too wordy, and too boring. Before the Assembly had concluded, Rancé—now just about thirty—had folded his tent, like the Arabs, and stolen silently away to his beloved Véretz.

By this time he had met and fallen in love with Marie d'Avaugour, duchesse de Montbazon, a statuesque and wholly immoral beauty at least fourteen years older than Rancé.[5] She was the wife of Hercule de Rohan, duc de Montbazon—he was in his sixties when they married—and she bore him a son and two daughters. She was a tall woman and possessed that indefinable something that made her irresistibly attractive to many men. Nor was she miserly with her favors. Cardinal de Retz, who was not unacquainted with such things, said that "she loved only her own pleasure and, above and beyond her pleasure, her own interests. I have never seen anyone who preserved in vice so little respect for virtue."[6] Her proclivities were well known, and in his *Historiettes* (a long series of short biographies), Gédéon Tallemant des Réaux reproduces an obscene street song that satirizes both the size of her body and the size of her carnal appetites.[7]

When and under what circumstances she and Rancé first met is unknown, but there is no doubt that he adored her, and the efforts of a number of well-meaning admirers of Rancé to show that their relationship was entirely platonic may be regarded as no more than wishful thinking. He still loved her in April 1657 when she contracted *la rougeole*, which might have been measles or might have been scarlet fever (both of which were far more dangerous in her day than in ours[8]), and died after just a few days. At the time of her unexpected death,

---

[5] For a more detailed account of Madame de Montbazon, see Bell, *Understanding Rancé*, 176–90.

[6] Cardinal de Retz, *Mémoires*, ed. Maurice Allem (Paris: Pléiade–Gallimard, 1956), 157.

[7] See Bell, *Understanding Rancé*, 182, n. 56.

[8] See David N. Bell, "Daniel de Larroque, Armand-Jean de Rancé, and the Head of Madame de Montbazon," *Cîteaux – Commentarii cistercienses* 53 (2002): 315–17.

Rancé was at Véretz and had planned to go to Paris to meet her. This he did, but exactly what happened then is not entirely clear. One of the commonest stories in circulation at the time had its origins in a small and scurrilous volume, published anonymously in 1685, with the title *Les Véritables motifs de la Conversion de l'abbé de la Trappe, avec quelques réflexions sur sa vie & sur ses écrits, ou Les Entretiens de Timocrate & de Philandre sur le livre qui a pour titre Les S. Devoirs de la Vie Monastique.*[9] The actual author was Daniel de Larroque (ca. 1660–1731),[10] and most of the book is taken up with attacks on a number of controversial passages from Rancé's *magnum opus, De la sainteté et des devoirs de la vie monastique,* published two years earlier in 1683.[11]

According to Larroque, once Rancé had reached Paris (still in ignorance of the duchess's death), he hastened to her town-house

> and went straight up to the duchess's chamber that he had permission to enter at any time. But instead of the delights he had anticipated, the first thing he saw was her coffin. That it awaited his mistress was obvious, since he was confronted with the sight of her bloody head, which, by chance, had rolled from under a cloth that had been carelessly thrown over it. It had been severed from the body at the neck so as to avoid the need to make a new and longer coffin. The one that had been made had been so poorly measured that it was six inches too short.[12]

This gruesome tale of the short coffin appears to have been a product of Larroque's imagination, but the tale itself may not be without foundation. The duchess, as we have said, had

---

[9] See Bell, *Understanding Rancé,* 314–15; *Les Véritables motifs . . .* (Cologne: Pierre Marteau, 1685).

[10] See Bell, *Understanding Rancé,* 147–49.

[11] See Bell, *Understanding Rancé,* 263–68.

[12] Larroque, *Véritables motifs,* 27–28; Bell, *Understanding Rancé,* 184.

died suddenly and unexpectedly, and there was almost certainly an autopsy. In Rancé's time, the removal of the head was a common part of the procedure, and autopsies might be carried out not in a hospital, but in a private dwelling.[13] It is therefore possible that, by some ghastly mischance, Rancé did indeed stumble across the corpse of his deceased mistress, and that her head had indeed been removed during the post mortem.[14] This cannot be regarded as certain, but neither can it be regarded as impossible. Whatever the facts of the case, there is no doubt that the death of the duchess proved a turning point in Rancé's life. It was not, in fact, the only thing that led to his conversion, and that conversion had not been as sudden as Larroque implies, but it unquestionably played a significant role.

Following the duchess's death, Rancé retired to Véretz and took the first definitive steps that would lead him, some six years later, to his taking vows as a novice at the Cistercian abbey of Perseigne on June 13, 1663. Those six years had not been idle. Rancé had consulted a number of people, both men and women, seeking their advice and encouragement. He had made two tours of the benefices he had inherited from his brother, Denis-François, one of them being la Trappe, which he found to be in appalling condition, both morally and physically. He began to divest himself of his other properties, including selling his beloved Véretz. Having determined, finally, to enter la Trappe as regular (not commendatory) abbot, he arranged for a great deal of necessary rebuilding and restoration. He spent the months from September 1662 to January 1663 at the abbey, overseeing the progress of the work, and this seems to have provided him with the final confirmation he needed that God was leading him to the Cistercian path—and not just

---

[13] See Bell, "Daniel de Larroque," 312–14.

[14] For a full and detailed discussion of the story of Madame de Montbazon's head, see Bell, "Daniel de Larroque," 305–31.

the Cistercian path, but the Cistercian path of the Strict Observance.[15]

Rancé's novitiate at Perseigne lasted a year—that was standard at the time—and it proved a shattering experience, both physically and spiritually. But Rancé was iron-willed, and his determination never wavered. Thus, on July 14, 1664, he entered la Trappe as its regular abbot (not without opposition from the half-dozen monks still in residence) and began the second part of his life.

He governed the house from July 1664 to May 1695, a period of just less than thirty-two years, when ill health forced him to resign. But he had been at the abbey for only six weeks when the superiors of the Strict Observance sent him to Rome to plead the cause of the Strict Observance in what has been called the War of the Observances.[16] He was there for eighteen months and did not enjoy it, nor was his mission a success. He was more than happy to return to la Trappe in May 1666 and, save for short absences on official business, never left the abbey again.

Rancé's time as abbot was not easy. Some of the difficulties he faced were made for him; some he made for himself. His monks, however, seem to have loved him, and there can be no doubt that he loved them. Their spiritual welfare was ever his deepest concern; their physical welfare was not. The grim mortality of la Trappe gained a certain unwanted notoriety,[17] though Rancé's logic was inexorable. It was also the logic of

---

[15] It is not quite accurate to use the terms "Strict" and "Common" Observance at this time, but it is certainly convenient: see further Bell, *Understanding Rancé*, 60–70. The standard account of the rise of the Strict Observance is Louis J. Lekai, *The Rise of the Cistercian Strict Observance in Seventeenth-Century France* (Washington, DC: The Catholic University of America Press, 1968). This is a brilliant study, but biased. Father Lekai was a member of the Common Observance, now called the Order of Cîteaux, and did not much care for the Strict Observance.

[16] Such is the title of Chapter XI in Louis J. Lekai's *The Cistercians: Ideals and Reality* (Kent, OH: Kent State University Press, 1977).

[17] See Bell, *Understanding Rancé*, 109–10, 223–24.

Saint Bernard. "Monks," said the saint (and Rancé quotes him), "have not been instructed in the school of Hippocrates and Galen, who teach the preservation of life, but in that of Jesus Christ, who tells us to lose it. This is a maxim that should be graven on the heart of everyone who has renounced the world in order to carry the cross of Jesus Christ in a life of withdrawal."[18] Rancé himself leaves us in no doubt:

> Solitaries, as we have said so many times, do not come to monasteries to live, but to die, and they should be neither surprised nor frightened to see frequent deaths. What they seek is the salvation of their souls, not the preservation of their life and health.[19]

Beyond the cloister walls, Rancé's abbacy was marked by controversy. There was, inevitably, an on-going and unresolvable dispute with the superiors of the Common Observance, who were, by definition, opposed to his reforms. Rancé himself had been deeply influenced by a volume written by Julien Paris, abbot of Foucarmont in Normandy, with the title *Du premier esprit de l'ordre de Cisteaux*.[20] It was first published in 1653 with two later enlarged editions in 1664 and 1670, and it seems fairly certain that Rancé first came across it during his novitiate at Perseigne. And what was the *premier esprit* of the Cistercian Order? The answer, according to Julien Paris, was simple and obvious: it was the meticulous and whole-hearted observance of the Rule of Saint Benedict. It follows logically, then, that if by Julien Paris's time the Order had become decadent and observance of the Rule lax (which was so), the Order could be

---

[18] Bernard, SC 30.4–5; SBOp 1:216–17; David N. Bell, *A Saint in the Sun: Praising Saint Bernard in the France of Louis XIV*, CS 271 (Collegeville, MN: Cistercian Publications, 2017), 175. This is cited in §33 of Rancé's conference for the feast day of Saint Bernard.

[19] Armand-Jean de Rancé, *De la sainteté et des devoirs de la vie monastique* (Paris: François Muguet, 1683), 2:459–60, quoted in Bell, *Understanding Rancé*, 223.

[20] For a summary of the book, see Bell, *Understanding Rancé*, 128–32.

restored and re-formed—literally re-formed, formed again—by re-establishing the Rule as the basis and foundation of monastic life.

With this view Rancé was in complete agreement, and although his approach to the Rule was more subtle and more nuanced than some have suggested, its strict observance became the foundation of his reform. Rancé's own *La Règle de saint Benoist, nouvellement traduite et expliquée selon son véritable esprit*,[21] which first appeared in 1688, is clearly indebted to the work of Julien Paris. In Rancé's eyes, the Common Observance had introduced far too many dispensations and mitigations into the Rule, especially in the matter of diet, and he had no time for any of them.

If the foundation of the reform was the Rule, the foundation of the Rule was humility. Chapter seven of the Rule sets out twelve steps of humility that form a Jacob's ladder leading from earth to heaven, from a love of self to that perfect love of God that casts out fear. As Augustine had said many centuries earlier, there are three parts to the path that leads to truth: the first part is humility, the second part is humility, and the third part is humility.[22] Humility, therefore, is essential, but what methods may an abbot legitimately use to instill it into his monks? The answer to this question gave rise to a long and bitter controversy between Rancé and one of his former friends, Guillaume Le Roy, commendatory abbot of Haute-Fontaine. In earlier and happier days Le Roy had spent time with Rancé at Véretz shortly after the death of Madame de Montbazon, and had been welcomed at la Trappe in June 1671. All that was to change.

At la Trappe, one of the techniques for training a monk involved what were technically known as humiliations. "A vigilant and loving superior," wrote Rancé, "will take care to train

---

[21] See Bell, *Understanding Rancé*, 270–75. But "despite his own rigorism, Rancé realized that, although much of the Rule must remain immutable, there are certain areas where changes could and should be made" (133).

[22] Augustine, *Epistola* 118.iii.22; PL 33:442.

a monk by reproaches, sharp reproofs, stinging words, public embarrassment, hard work, and degrading occupations,"[23] and even if a monk tries to do well, the superior will always find something wrong to criticize. This could easily be misunderstood as involving the deliberate invention of non-existent faults—the technical term here was "fictions"—in which case the superior would be lying, which is a serious sin. This was exactly how humiliations were understood by Guillaume Le Roy, and it led to a long-drawn-out and wordy conflict between him and Rancé that began in about 1671 and lasted for almost a decade. Neither side came out particularly well, and the spirit of Christian charity was noticeable by its absence. Rancé, we might add, had not invented the idea of humiliations, but had borrowed it from John Climacus, John of the Ladder, a sixth/ seventh-century ascetic who had a deep influence on the formation of Rancé's spirituality.

About another decade was taken up in an even nastier quarrel with Dom Innocent Le Masson, General of the Carthusians. This lasted from 1683 to 1692 (officially), and the question at issue was whether the Carthusians could or could not justly be accused of laxity. In his *De la sainteté et des devoirs de la vie monastique* there were certain passages in which Rancé had contrasted the asceticism and austerity of the earliest Carthusians with what he considered a more lax approach in Le Masson's own times. Le Masson was infuriated. He and Rancé were much alike in many ways—devout, austere, learned, not a little self-righteous—and Le Masson was ready to take offence at the slightest whiff of criticism of his beloved Order. Thus, in 1683, Le Masson published a long and extremely critical refutation of Rancé's comments that included some highly critical comments on Rancé himself.[24] It was an intemperate attack, and in 1689 Rancé, alas, replied just as intemperately with a long letter pointing out in no uncertain terms

---

[23] Rancé, *De la sainteté*, 1:314, quoted in Bell, *Understanding Rancé*, 125.
[24] See Bell, *Understanding Rancé*, 146.

how, why, and where Dom Innocent was wrong.[25] The quarrel degenerated from bad to worse, and although it was officially ended by royal command in 1689 (the king imposed silence on both parties), it was still sizzling under the surface seven years later.

Finally, again for about a decade, there was the controversy with the learned Maurist Dom Jean Mabillon on the question of monastic studies. This lasted from 1684 to 1693, and the question was simple: what should a monk read and what books should a monastic library contain? Putting the matter as briefly as possible, Rancé wholly supported reading and study for the purposes of transformation (basically *lectio divina*), but had no time for reading and study simply for the purposes of information. Erudition, he says—and by erudition he means learning for the sake of learning, or, more accurately, studying theology for the sake of theology—erudition

> is the reef on which humility founders, and vanity, which is the most common result of study, has often inflicted a thousand mortal wounds on the hearts of scholars who, despite all their enlightenment, were not even aware of what was going wrong.[26]

Mabillon, on the other hand, held the view that the labor of the mind could be used for the greater glory of God, and that there could be a true spirituality of scholasticism. It could be seen, for example, in both Aquinas and Bonaventure, and, for Mabillon and his confrères, it was the Maurist tradition. There was no right or wrong, therefore, in the dispute between Mabillon and Rancé—the two were arguing from different premises—but it must be said that throughout the long and

---

[25] See Bell, *Understanding Rancé*, 146–47.

[26] *Pensée* 207 in Part Two (the Translation), quoting Rancé's letter of October 5, 1680, to an unknown Benedictine (the beginning of the letter is lost): *Abbé de Rancé: Correspondance*, ed. Alban J. Krailsheimer, 4 vols. (Paris: Cîteaux-Le Cerf, 1993), 2:434.

(as usual) wordy dispute, Mabillon always retained a gentlemanly courtesy that one does not always find in Rancé.[27]

These were the principal disputes—there were others of lesser consequence—that occupied much of Rancé's time as abbot. It cannot be said that they display him at his best. But his continual labors and ardent asceticism took their toll. By 1694 he was suffering severely from gastric problems, partly because of the rigorous fasting and meager diet at the abbey and partly as a result of a rupture he had sustained a number of years earlier while working in the fields. He was also suffering from severe rheumatism or rheumatoid arthritis, and the incessant pain gave him no rest either by day or night. Both his legs were swollen and inflamed, as was his right hand, so much so that he could no longer sign his letters. Finally, when he was unable to walk without assistance, he had no choice but to enter the infirmary at la Trappe, and in May of the following year he resigned as abbot. He lived on to see three successors: first Dom Zozime Foisil, who died unexpectedly in March 1696, second Dom Armand-François Gervaise, an erratic and turbulent monk who deserves a biography to himself and who was forced to resign in 1698, and third Dom Jacques de La Cour, who became abbot in April 1699 and was with Rancé when he died.[28] Death claimed Rancé between one and two o'clock in the afternoon of Wednesday, October 27, 1700. He was seventy-four, and lucid until his very last moment. He was given the last rites by Monseigneur Louis d'Aquin, bishop of Séez, who has left us an account of Rancé's last hours.[29]

---

[27] See further Bell, *Understanding Rancé*, 111–14. There is now a considerable bibliography on the controversy over monastic studies, but, in my opinion, the best study remains that by Henri Didio, *La querelle de Mabillon et de l'Abbé de Rancé* (Amiens: Rousseau–Leroy, 1892). This is a sober, readable, balanced account, with a wealth of documentation. The much more recent study by Blandine Barrett-Kriegel, *La querelle Mabillon-Rancé* (Paris: Quai Voltaire, 1992), adds nothing, is sometimes wrong, and may safely be ignored.

[28] See Charles-Félix-Hyacinthe, comte de Charencey, *Histoire de l'abbaye de la Grande-Trappe* (Mortagne, 1896–1911), 1:327–52.

[29] See Bell, *Understanding Rancé*, 324, for details.

He was always a controversial figure, and generally evoked feelings of either love or loathing—there was no grey area—something that is reflected in the numerous biographies of Rancé. The earliest are all adulatory and reflect a concerted movement to have Rancé canonized. As it happened, this came to nothing, not because of any vicious opposition, but because times and circumstances changed, and the attempt simply fizzled out. The biographies that followed vary from spiteful criticism to further adulation,[30] albeit somewhat tempered, and it was not until 1974 that we find, for the first time, a fair and balanced assessment, based on a careful examination of the original sources, of the life and works, both inside and outside the cloister, of the abbot of la Trappe. This was Professor Alban Krailsheimer's *Armand-Jean de Rancé, Abbot of La Trappe: His Influence in the Cloister and the World.*[31] In 1993 Professor Krailsheimer followed this with an excellent four-volume edition of Rancé's correspondence,[32] thus providing us with an indispensable source for understanding the development of Rancé's thought and spirituality.

For the purposes of this present volume, we shall be concerned with no more than two of these (too) many biographies, that by Jacques Marsollier, first published in 1703, and that by Philippe-Irenée Boistel d'Exauvillez, first published in 1842. They are the only two that contain the *Pensées* that are the subject of this study. The third version of the *Pensées*, published in 1767 under the title *Pensées et réflexions de M. de Rancé, Abbé de la Trappe*, did not appear in any biography, but as a separate volume in its own right. So who were Marsollier and Boistel d'Exauvillez? That is a matter for our next chapter.

---

[30] For a discussion of the biographies and biographers, see Bell, *Understanding Rancé*, chap. 1, Rancé's Biographers.

[31] See n. 1 above.

[32] Krailshemer, *Abbé de Rancé: Correspondance.*

Chapter Two

Jacques Marsollier and the Publication of the *Pensées*

We must begin, briefly, with a few words about an earlier biographer, Pierre de Maupeou. As a young man he had tried his vocation at la Trappe, but had been forced to abandon his design for reasons of health. He went on to become the parish priest of Nonancourt in the diocese of Évreux, about fifty kilometers east of la Trappe. While at the abbey, Maupeou had begun to collect documents that would support the movement for Rancé's canonization, and he was a man wholly devoted to Rancé and his memory. In 1685 he had already published a reply to Daniel de Larroque's *Véritables motifs* (it was quite ineffective, and Larroque's work was far more readable), and after Rancé's death he published an *Éloge funèbre* at the request of Reverend Mother Françoise-Angélique d'Étampes de Valençay, abbess of les Clairets, a woman of great authority who was equally devoted to Rancé and his memory.[1]

Then, in 1702, Maupeou produced in two volumes what was really the first biography of Rancé: *La vie du Très-Révérend Père Armand-Jean Le Bouthillier de Rancé, Abbé & Réformateur du monastère de la Trappe*. He had been working on the book for

---

[1] For bibliographical details of Maupeou's attack on Larroque and his *Éloge funèbre*, see David N. Bell, *Understanding Rancé: The Spirituality of the Abbot of La Trappe in Context*, CS 205 (Kalamazoo, MI: Cistercian Publications, 2005), 315, 325–26.

some time, and although it includes material that cannot be found elsewhere, it cannot be called reliable. Given its association with the canonization process, it tends to be hagiographical, and in areas where Maupeou did not have documentary sources, he was not averse to using his own imagination. Ailbe Luddy, a monk/priest of Mount Melleray Abbey in Ireland, writing in 1931, had nothing good at all to say of Maupeou's biography. "He showed," wrote Luddy, "that he had neither the knowledge nor the judgment required for the undertaking, and his two volumes rather injured than honoured his hero."[2]

Meanwhile, another monk of la Trappe had been accumulating material for a more complete life of Rancé. This was Jean-Baptiste de La Tour, prior of the abbey, who had entered la Trappe in 1695. He interviewed as many of the older members of the community as he could and made careful copies of whatever relevant documents he could find, especially letters to and from Rancé. His own ill health prevented him from completing his task, and his projected life of Rancé was never finished. The material he gathered, however, did not go to waste.

Given that Maupeou's life was unreliable, and given that La Tour's health had put an end to his own labors, it was clear that there was still need for a new and more accurate life of the abbot. Thus, at the very beginning of the eighteenth century, some one or some group contacted Jacques Marsollier, archdeacon of Uzès (far away in the south of France, about twenty-five kilometers north-northeast of Nîmes), and commissioned him to compose the new life that was clearly needed. According to the *Bulletin du bibliophile* for 1867, speaking on the authority of Dom Jean-Armand Gervaise, it was a Jansenist or Jansenizing group that contacted Marsollier and paid him three thousand *livres* for his work.[3] To assist him in his task, he was given access to certain "Mémoires de la Trappe" com-

---

[2] Ailbe J. Luddy, *The Real de Rancé: Illustrious Penitent and Reformer of Notre Dame de la Trappe* (London and New York: Longmans Green & Co., 1931), 312.
[3] *Bulletin du bibliophile et du bibliothécaire* 33 (1867): 214.

piled by "a learned religious," that can only have been the notes collected by La Tour for his own unfinished *Life*. But why Marsollier?

Jacques Marsollier was born in Paris in 1647 and, after the usual schooling, became a regular canon at the great Parisian abbey of Sainte-Geneviève. He later moved south, where he was appointed archdeacon of Uzès, and it was there and in that role that he died in 1724. He was a professional historian and the author of numerous biographies, none of them more than mediocre in quality and some of them gravely inaccurate. There were lives of Cardinal Ximenez, Henry VII of England, Francis de Sales, Henri de La Tour d'Auvergne, and Jeanne de Chantal, as well as a history of ecclesiastical tithing, a history of the Inquisition, and a flawed apology for Erasmus. But his books were well written—they are what we would call an easy read—and often reprinted. In other words, Marsollier was a well-known and popular historian who could be trusted (by those who did not know better) to write a sound biography of the abbot of la Trappe. And so he did. His *La vie de Dom Armand-Jean Le Bouthillier de Rancé, Abbé régulier et Réformateur du Monastère de la Trappe, de l'Étroite Observance de Cisteaux* was first published by Jean de Nully at Paris in 1703. It appeared first as a single quarto, and then, in the same year, as two duodecimos. A new edition, also in two volumes, appeared in 1758.[4] It was not well received by the Cistercians, either at la Trappe or in general, for it sought to show that Rancé had strong and unequivocal sympathies with Jansenism—and we must remember that it may well have been Jansenist sympathizers who paid for the book. The general chapter of 1835 prohibited its reading.

The first of the two duodecimos opens with an engraving of the famous portrait of Rancé by Hyacinthe Rigaud,[5] a dedicatory letter to King Louis XIV, and an interesting foreword in

---

[4] See Bell, *Understanding Rancé*, 326–27.
[5] Reproduced as a frontispiece in Bell, *Understanding Rancé*.

which Marsollier tells us something of how he prepared his biography and summarizes the contents of its six books. The last chapter, ending on page 460, brings to a close book three, which deals with the establishment of the reform at the abbey and the central importance of the penitential life. The second volume opens with the aftermath of the general chapter of 1667, takes us through Rancé's life and writings both inside and outside the cloister, and ends on page 478, as we might expect, with his death and a commendation of his virtues.

But then, in an appendix of 83 pages with its own numeration, we find the *Pensées de l'abbé de la Trappe sur divers sujets de piété. Tirées de ses Lettres Spirituelles*, "Thoughts of the Abbot of la Trappe on Various Subjects of Piety, Taken from his Spiritual Letters," which are the subject of this present volume. Marsollier explains what he has done and why he has done it in a two-page foreword to the *Pensées*, and we cannot do better than to let him say what he said in his own words:

Foreword[6]

The collection of thoughts that follow this foreword has been compiled by the author of this biography to serve the spirit of the abbot of la Trappe. He has taken them from a number of [the abbot's] *Spiritual Letters* that have not yet been made available to the public. The short time he was given to complete his work did not allow him to provide as complete an account of the spirit of this great solitary as he had planned, and it was not possible for him to make as much use of [the Letters] as he had intended. Some pious and knowledgeable people, however, expressed a desire to see them, and, having found them so fine and useful, they advised him to offer them to the public just as they are. They added that nothing could make one better aware of the height and breadth of the spirit and preeminent piety of the abbot of la Trappe than the thoughts contained in this collection.

---

[6] Marsollier, *Vie de Rancé*, 1–2 (1703 ed.); 499–500 (1758 ed.).

To these arguments the author objected that there was a lack of order and continuity in the Thoughts, but they replied that the Thoughts of the late Monsieur Pascal[7] had not failed to please the public and had been of infinite use to them, even though they had neither more order nor more continuity than the Thoughts of the abbot of la Trappe.

On thinking this over, the author resolved to have them printed. His wish is that the public will take from them all that useful guidance they might expect from a heart as pure and a spirit as illumined as that of the abbot of la Trappe.

There are 259 *Pensées*,[8] ranging in length from a couple of lines to about thirty, though anything over twenty lines is rare. They are all numbered in Roman numerals, and each has a subtitle briefly summarizing its content. Sometimes the summary is no more than a single word. The collection also appears at the end of the second volume of the *nouvelle edition* of 1758, but the pagination is now continuous with the rest of the volume, and the subtitles have been moved to the margins.

The first edition of the *Pensées* appeared, as we have seen, in 1703 as a separately paginated appendix to Marsollier's Life, but so far as I am aware, it was never published as a separate volume. This changed in 1767 when an anonymous editor brought out a new version that was indeed published as a separate volume under the title *Pensées et réflexions de M. de Rancé, Abbé de la Trappe*.[9] It is a neat duodecimo of 156 pages, with an engraving of Rigaud's portrait of Rancé at the beginning, and

---

[7] Pascal died in 1662 and left a collection of fragments, some more complete, some less complete, of what he intended to be an *apologia* for Christianity. These were collected together after his death and published as his *Pensées* in 1670. The first edition of Marsollier's *Life* appeared in 1703. Pascal's *Pensées* had certainly not failed to please the public, because of both their content and their exquisite French.

[8] There is some misnumbering in both editions. The 1703 edition ends with *Pensée* 258; the 1758 edition with *Pensée* 256. The details will become clear in the notes to the translation.

[9] Published by Chez Vente at Paris: see Bell, *Understanding Rancé*, 310.

a new and interesting foreword that we shall examine in a moment. In this little volume, the *Pensées* occupy pages 5 to 115, but are then followed (pages 116–56) by a *Paraphrase sur les sept pseaumes de la pénitence*, which, though beautifully written, is not here our concern.

The new foreword, however, is certainly interesting. The anonymous editor begins by giving a brief account of the life and dramatic conversion of Rancé, though he errs in calling him Jean-Armand rather than Armand-Jean, and his story of Rancé's conversion is entirely dependent on Daniel de Larroque, either by reading him or by popular hearsay. He is right, then, in saying that Rancé was on intimate terms with Madame de Montbazon, and he is right when he tells us that she died, suddenly and unexpectedly, when Rancé was at his country estate at Véretz. As we saw in chapter one, he had returned to Paris to meet her before the news of her death reached him, and when he made his way to her chamber at her Paris residence, it was to find the hideous sight of her dead body with the head separated from it. The editor of the *Pensées* now follows Larroque in narrating, once again, the gruesome tale of the embalmers cutting off the head of the duchess because the coffin prepared for her was too short. Here, then, is a translation of the editor's foreword:

Editor's Foreword[10]

The *Thoughts* that comprise this little collection are taken from the Spiritual Letters of the celebrated JEAN-ARMAND[11] LE BOUTHILLIER DE RANCÉ, abbot of la Trappe. As we know, he spent his youth at the [Royal] Court, where he indulged himself in all the enticing attractions this world has to offer, and was then

---

[10] *Pensées et réflexions*, 1–4.

[11] This is incorrect. As we saw in chap. 1, he was christened Armand-Jean in honor of his illustrious godfather, Armand-Jean du Plessis, Cardinal de Richelieu. We might also note that after he entered la Trappe, Rancé ceased to use the family name Le Bouthillier.

called to a life of religious observance and piety by one of those scenes of death that the divine mercy sometimes uses to lay low hardened sinners and confirm the faith of the elect.

[¹²The abbé de Rancé did not know of the sickness and death of Madame the Duchess de Montbazon, with whom he had been very intimate, and he comes to see her. At her residence he climbs a secret stair, and the first thing he sees is the head of this famous beauty that those responsible for embalming her corpse had separated from her body because the lead coffin had been found to be too short.]

This was the moment and lightning-flash of grace. In a whirl of thoughts he saw how dreadful and unexpected purposes can arise in our soul, he saw that the most glorious career can be halted in mid-stream, and that his only sure course was to follow the advice of the Apostle, namely, to use the things of this world as if one did not use them, for the form [of this world] is passing away.¹³ Now, happily, he reflected seriously on his way of life, and, in the bitterness in which he was being plunged by this salutary compunction, he cried out, "Alas! Perhaps the same stroke will fall on my head! Perhaps I will end up by repeating these doleful sighs of [King] Hezekiah: *Ego dixi in dimidio dierum meorum vadam ad portas inferi.*¹⁴ What then will be my recourse before the sovereign Judge? What account shall I render to him? O deadly world, I am done with you! I break all the bonds that bound me to you; my eyes are opened, and all they see now is your deceitfulness. From this moment on I dedicate myself to penitence for as many days as the divine condescension will leave me."

This courageous resolve was not the effect of fear alone; it was inspired and sustained by grace, and the abbé de Rancé immediately hastened to bury himself in the solitude, and, once there, he wished to have as his companions only those men who were as convinced as he that they had to atone for a worldly life, soft and fastidious, by undertaking every austerity and priva-

---

¹² This paragraph in square brackets appears as a footnote on pages 1–2 of the *Pensées et réflexions*. We discussed the story in chap. 1.

¹³ 1 Cor 7:31.

¹⁴ Isa 38:10: "In the midst of my days I shall go to the gates of hell."

tion that mortal men could endure, without absolutely killing themselves.

Those same ideas that, after his withdrawal from the world, continually guided the way of life of the abbot of la Trappe, and that lead us to revere his memory, shine forth here in every way. We see everywhere that submission to Providence, that denial of oneself, that heartfelt confidence of a devout soul in the divine mercy, that wholesome fear that is the beginning of true wisdom,[15] that constant determination to destroy the old self so as to clothe oneself in the new,[16] that perfect abandonment of one's own will so as to have no other but that of the heavenly Father, and, finally, that anointing and odor of salvation breathed in by souls that are truly fearful. To all these admirable characteristics, this work adds the noblest and most appropriate style for its sublime purpose, and it is, we believe, a true gift to the public.

The third and, I think, the final time that the *Pensées* appear in print is in the biography of Rancé published for the first time in 1842 by Philippe-Irenée Boistel d'Exauvillez.[17] We have moved on about sixty-five years from the *Pensées et réflexions.* The author was born in Amiens on 6 December 1786 and was the grandson of Boistel d'Welles, who had occupied a number of senior posts in both the national and local administration, and who was a member of the Académie d'Amiens. Events associated with the Bourbon Restoration of 1814–1815 resulted in the loss of much of the family fortune, and Boistel d'Exauvillez left Amiens for Paris. His attempts at finding employment appropriate to his station were not particularly successful, and he then devoted himself to literature. He himself was a deeply religious man of irreproachable morality, and he dedicated his pen to the defense of the Catholic religion and the moral instruction of the young. His works were numerous

---

[15] Ps 110:10; Prov 9:10.

[16] Eph 4:22-24.

[17] My account of Boistel d'Exauvillez is dependent on the entry in Charles Louandre and Félix Bourquelot, *La littérature française contemporaine, 1827–1844* (Paris: Delaroque Aîné, 1846), 2:159–62.

and well received,[18] and his historical writings included lives of Saint Peter and Saint Paul; Hyacinthe-Louis de Quélen, archbishop of Paris from 1821 to 1839; Godefroy de Bouillon, one of the leaders of the First Crusade and the first ruler of the Kingdom of Jerusalem; and—our particular interest here—Armand-Jean de Rancé. The last two belonged to the series *Gloires de la France*, the volumes of which were published under the direction of Boistel d'Exauvillez. Under this title, we are told, "M. d'Exauvillez has gathered together the lives of famous people who, by their virtues, their actions, or their writings, have truly created the glory of our country: religious glory, political glory, military glory, literary glory. It is our business to emulate their accomplishments."[19]

The first edition of the *Histoire de l'abbé de Rancé, réformateur de la Trappe* appeared in 1842, but a new edition, "revised, corrected, and enlarged by the abbé R. Bonhomme, priest of the diocese of Évreux," was published in 1868.[20] This took into account the important work of Louis Dubois, *Histoire de l'abbé de Rancé et de sa réforme*, which was first published in two substantial volumes in 1866.[21] Boistel d'Exauvillez reproduces the *Pensées* of Marsollier, but, as he tells us in his introduction to the collection, he has re-organized them according to subject matter:

> If the life of the abbot of Rancé offers us one of the most perfect examples of Christian penitence, his writings are no less precious on account of the wise advice and lofty teachings contained within them. We think we would have left our task but half done had we not given the reader the opportunity of appreciating the holy abbot by means of this

[18] Louandre and Bourquelot list forty-eight titles under *Ouvrages de religion* (7 titles), *Ouvrages moraux pour l'instruction de la jeunesse* (32 titles), and *Histoire et Biographie* (10 titles).

[19] *L'Ami de religion: Journal ecclésiastique, politique et littéraire* 114 (1842): 503.

[20] See Bell, *Understanding Rancé*, 17–18, 337–38.

[21] See Bell, *Understanding Rancé*, 16–17.

new account. To this end, the various thoughts and maxims that here follow were taken from his Spiritual Letters and here classified, so far as their nature permitted, by subject matter. For the most part, they do not have that brilliance that sometimes dazzles more than it illuminates, and they are as simple as the heart that inspired them. Yet they possess a solidity and perfume of piety that can only render their knowledge most useful to the public, and justify in super-abundance the place we have given, in the *Glories of France*, to this hero of Christian penitence, no less commendable by his talents than by his virtues.[22]

The author classes the *Pensées* under eleven headings: (1) the need to despise the world and value only eternity, (2) afflictions and suffering, (3) trust in God, (4) submission to God, (5) love of God and one's neighbor, (6) the use and abuse of graces, (7) the need for works, (8) delusions and aberrations of the human spirit, (9) the danger of delaying one's conversion,[23] (10) the necessity and benefits of prayer, and (11) miscellaneous thoughts (*pensées detachées*). All in all, and as we shall see, it is an accurate summary of the main themes of the *Pensées*.

It is time now to move towards an examination of the *Pensées* themselves and determine whether and to what extent they represent, as Marsollier says, "the spirit of the abbot of la Trappe." But in order to do that we need to give a brief account

---

[22] Philippe-Irenée Boistel d'Exauvillez, *Histoire de l'abbé de Rancé, réformateur de la Trappe* (Paris: Librairie de Debécourt, 1842), 383–84.

[23] *Conversion*, the same word in both French and English, is the *conversatio morum* of the Rule of Saint Benedict 58.17. It involves, essentially, detaching ourselves from the transitory and alluring things of this world and attaching ourselves to the unchangeable things that pertain to eternity. It is to change our direction from this world to the world to come, from *temporalia* to *spiri-tualia*, from the creature to the Creator. *Conversion* might therefore be trans-lated by "changing one's way of life." For Rancé (whose own conversion was nothing if not dramatic), the most effective conversion also involved leaving the world for the silent solitude of the monastery. Marsollier makes it clear that although this may be the ideal, conversion is an obligation for every Christian and applies to every man and every woman.

of Rancé's spirituality as it appears in his own writings, not in selected excerpts, and in order to do *that* we need first to say a few words about the nature of spirituality and its relationship to mysticism.

Chapter Three

Spirituality without Mysticism

According to Paul Clogan, spirituality "is a subject upon which an inordinate amount of nonsense has been and continues to be written."[1] As the term is used today, *spirituality* is a word of recent coinage. It is not quite as recent as some have supposed, but in its sense of "attachment to or regard for things of the spirit as opposed to material or worldly interests,"[2] it dates in English from the first decades of the sixteenth century. Its association with interiority, infused grace, and experiential knowledge came later—from the seventeenth century in France and the nineteenth in England—although in both countries the main diffusion of the term dates from the second decade of the twentieth century.[3] As Sandra Schneiders has said, by the eighteenth century the term *spirituality*

> was used to refer to the life of perfection as distinguished from the "ordinary" life of faith, and the role of the spiritual

[1] Paul M. Clogan, preface to *Medievalia et Humanistica: Studies in Medieval and Renaissance Culture, New Series, Number 4: Medieval and Renaissance Spirituality* (Denton: Rowman & Littlefield, 1973), vii.

[2] *Oxford English Dictionary*, 2nd ed. (Oxford: Oxford University Press, 1986), 16:259 (col. 3).

[3] See Aimé Solignac, "Spiritualité," in *Dictionnaire de spiritualité* (Paris: Beauchesne, 1990), 14:1146–50; Walter H. Principe, "Toward Defining Spirituality," *Studies in Religion/Sciences religieuses* 12 (1983): 130–35; and *The Study of Spirituality*, ed. Cheslyn Jones, Geoffrey Wainwright, and Edward Yarnold (Oxford: Oxford University Press, 1986), xxiv–xxvi.

director as the one who possessed the requisite theological expertise to guide the mystic (actual or potential) assumed great importance. By the 19th and early 20th centuries the meaning common just prior to the [Second Vatican] council, i.e. spirituality as the practice of the interior life by those oriented to the life of perfection, was firmly established.[4]

Modern definitions are legion, and this is not the place to discuss them,[5] but in general they tend to dwell on notions of "self-transcendence"[6] or "the inner dimension" of a person where he or she experiences "ultimate reality,"[7] or striving to achieve "the highest ideal or goal,"[8] and so on. In other words, they tend to dwell on the end of the spiritual path rather than the path itself. The tendency is not, of course, true of all writers—Geoffrey Wainwright, for example, is not alone in defining spirituality simply as "praying and living"[9]—but it is undoubtedly common. And even Geoffrey Wainwright cannot resist identifying spirituality with "mystical theology and with such parts of moral and ascetical theology as relate to it."[10] Other examples are too numerous to warrant discussion.

Robert Swanson has rightly pointed out the dangers of these approaches:

> Our squeamishness, and insistence on a definition of spirituality which tends to invalidate anything which does not

[4] Sandra M. Schneiders, "Spirituality in the Academy," *Theological Studies* 50 (1989): 681.

[5] See, for example, the entertaining paper by Stuart Rose, "Is the Term 'Spirituality' a Word that Everyone Uses, But Nobody Knows What Anyone Means by it?" *Journal of Contemporary Religion* 16 (2001): 193–207.

[6] See, for example, Michael Downey, *Understanding Christian Spirituality* (New York and Mahwah, NJ: Paulist Press, 1997), 14, 15, 32, 35, 46–48, 118, 125, 127–28.

[7] Ewert Cousins, "Preface to the Series," *Christian Spirituality: Origins to the Twelfth Century*, ed. Bernard McGinn, John Meyendorff, and Jean Leclercq (New York: Crossroad, 1985), xiii.

[8] Principe, "Toward Defining Spirituality," 139.

[9] Jones, et al., *Study of Spirituality*, 9, 604–5.

[10] Jones, et al., *Study of Spirituality*, xxii.

approach the mystical—and preferably the Dionysian version of mysticism through the penetration of the darkness surrounding an ineffable divinity, rather than that which offered an affective, emotion-centred and emotion-directed access to God—places a major barrier between the twentieth century and pre-Reformation religious practices.[11]

Is it possible, then, to have spirituality without mysticism? Certainly it is, but to appreciate this we must first turn our attention to the meaning of the Latin word *spiritualitas* not as we use it today, but as it was used in the Middle Ages. In this investigation the work of Aimé Solignac remains fundamental.[12] *Spiritualitas*, he finds, was never a word of common occurrence,[13] though it appeared more frequently than has sometimes been supposed, and in his admirable summary of the matter he identifies three main usages—religious, philosophical, and legal—that can be found in texts dating from the early fifth century to the end of the Middle Ages.

First, in the religious sense, *spiritualitas* stands in opposition to *carnalitas* or *animalitas*. This is an ancient idea—it can be seen in Plato—and in Christian theology it is characteristic of the writings of Saint Paul. The earliest occurrence of the word in this sense appears to be in a letter long attributed to Jerome, but actually written either by Pelagius or (more probably) one of his semi-Pelagian followers. Here, *spiritualitas* simply means holding to what is good and making progress (*proficere*) therein.[14] And since human beings alone possess rationality (*ratio-*

---

[11] Robert N. Swanson, *Catholic England: Faith, Religion and Observance Before the Reformation* (Manchester and New York: Manchester University Press, 1993), 22.

[12] See n. 3 above, and Solignac's "L'apparition du mot *spiritualitas* au Moyen Âge," *Bulletin du Cange, Archivum Latinitatis Medii Aevi* 44 (1985): 185–206. See also Jean Leclercq, "Spiritualitas," *Studi Medievali* 3 (1962): 279–96.

[13] We must remember, however, that while *spiritualitas* was not common, *spiritualis* and *spiritualiter* occur everywhere.

[14] *Ps.*-Jerome, *Epistola* VII.ix; PL 30:114D–15A. See Solignac, "L'apparition," 187–88, and "Spiritualité," 1143; and Principe, "Toward Defining Spirituality,"

nalitas), says Gilbert of Poitiers, and since without rationality we cannot distinguish between good and evil, it follows that *spiritualitas* is entirely a human—indeed, *the* human—characteristic.[15] Bruno the Carthusian contrasts *spiritualitas* with *sensualitas*, and says simply that *spiritualitas ad alta semper tendit*: "spirituality always strives for higher things."[16]

Second, in the philosophical or metaphysical sense, *spiritualitas* stands opposed to *carnalitas* and, as such, designates a mode of being or knowing. The physical bread and wine of the Eucharist, for example, are "corporeal," but once they have been transformed by the Holy Spirit into the body and blood of Christ, they belong to the realm of *spiritualitas*. This second contrast, essentially between spirit and matter, is particularly important for the scholastic writers,[17] though the scholastic usage of the word is not restricted to this. William of Auvergne, for example, defines *spiritualitas* as that "by which we remove from our souls spiritual evils, which are vices and sins . . . and seek to acquire for our souls spiritual goods, which are all the virtues and the gifts of grace."[18] This is precisely the thought of *ps.*-Jerome.

Third, in the legal sense, *spiritualitas* is the complement of *temporalitas*, in that "temporalities" refer to the temporal or physical possession of an ecclesiastical institution and the revenues derived therefrom (tithes being the obvious example), and "spiritualities" to the body of ecclesiastical persons, to

---

130, n. 19.

[15] Gilbert of Poitiers, *Exp. In Boetii lib. I de Trin.*, 2.77; *The Commentaries on Boethius by Gilbert of Poitiers*, ed. Nicholas M. Häring (Toronto: Pontifical Institute of Mediaeval Studies, 1966), 95.

[16] Bruno the Carthusian, *Exp. in Ps. 83*; PL 152:1083AB.

[17] See Solignac, "Spiritualité," 1143, 1145–46; and Jean Leclercq's introduction to *The Spirituality of Western Christendom*, ed. E. Rozanne Elder, CS 30 (Kalamazoo, MI: Cistercian Publications, 1976), xxix.

[18] William of Auvergne, *De anima*, V.xii; *Guillelmi Alverni Opera Omnia* (Paris: Denis Thierri, 1674; repr. Frankfurt am Main: Minerva, 1963), II/ii:130. See Solignac, "L'apparition," 202, and "Spiritualité," 1145.

ecclesiastical property, or to revenues held or received in return for spiritual services such as the administration of the sacraments. This is the earliest usage of the term in English, but it is not of major concern in our present discussion.

For our purposes, the first contrast, between *spiritualitas* and *carnalitas*, is the most important, and it is little more than Guibert of Nogent's idea that "spirituality" is living a life based on the teachings of the Christian Scriptures.[19] But simple and straightforward as this may be, what is of vital importance is that *spiritualitas* in this sense involves doing as much as being, outward action as much as inward meditation, and equally important is the fact that in the Middle Ages, and for many theologians at the time of Rancé, the division so commonly made nowadays between thought and action was far less clearly delineated. "For medieval people," writes Norman Tanner,

> there was far less of a distinction between the outer and inner aspects of religion than for us today. . . . Medieval people thought and expressed themselves largely by what they did, and therefore their external activities were the key to, indeed for the most part *were*, their inner piety.[20]

So where does the experiential, mystical knowledge of God stand in all this? For the theologians of the twelfth and much of the thirteenth century, the experiential knowledge of God was the proper culmination of *spiritualitas*, defined as "holding

---

[19] Guibert of Nogent, *De vita sua*, I, 17; PL 156:874AB; Solignac, "L'apparition," 192–94, "Spiritualité," 1144–45.

[20] Norman P. Tanner, "Piety in the Middle Ages," in *A History of Religion in Britain: Practice and Belief from Pre-Roman Times to the Present*, ed. Sheridan Gilley and W. J. Sheils (Oxford: Wiley-Blackwell, 1994), 71. See also page 75: "for mostly unlettered people, such as in late medieval England, piety chiefly consisted of their external religious activities, not something beyond or different from them."

to what is good and making progress therein,"[21] and of rational, human inquiry. We are, whether we like it or not, images of God, though seriously flawed by sin. And given that that image is to be found in the highest rational part of the human soul—that part that the plants and animals do not share—it is blasphemous not to use that gift to the best of our ability to come to some knowledge of that One in whose image we are created. It follows, then, that for the theologians of the twelfth and early thirteenth centuries,

> the pursuit of knowledge ennobles a man, for wisdom and science are reflections of eternal wisdom; they bring the lover of wisdom into an intimate communication with the most pure, divine Spirit. The true philosopher is he who rises to the vision of God over the ascending degrees of knowledge.[22]

Philosophy, in other words, was not intended to be a barren pandering to *curiositas*, a concept universally condemned by monastic writers,[23] but a way of transformation. Indeed, it was the conviction of the entire medieval spiritual tradition that one cannot understand the nature of God without becoming—so far as it is possible—what God is.[24] It is a theology of

[21] *Ps.*-Jerome, *Epistola* VII.ix; PL 30:114D–15A. See Solignac, "L'apparition," 187–88, and "Spiritualité," 1143; and Principe, "Toward Defining Spirituality," 130, n. 19.

[22] John P. Kleinz, *The Theory of Knowledge of Hugh of Saint Victor* (Washington, DC: Catholic University of America Press, 1944), 118.

[23] See A. Cabassut, "Curiosité," in *Dictionnaire de spiritualité* (Paris: Beauchesne, 1953), 2:2654–61; Richard Newhauser, "The Sin of Curiosity and the Cistercians," in *Erudition at God's Service: Studies in Medieval Cistercian History, XI*, ed. John R. Sommerfeldt, CS 98 (Kalamazoo, MI: Cistercian Publications, 1987), 71–95; William J. Courtenay, "Spirituality and Late Scholasticism," in *Christian Spirituality II: High Middle Ages and Reformation*, ed. Jill Raitt (New York: Crossroad, 1998), 114–17.

[24] See David N. Bell, *The Image and Likeness: The Augustinian Spirituality of William of Saint-Thierry*, CS 78 (Kalamazoo, MI: Cistercian Publications, 1984), chap. 5, *passim*.

connatural knowledge.[25] The principle is ultimately Platonic, but a common modern error is to suppose that becoming what God is refers only to the highest and most rarefied reaches of the mystical path. Nothing could be more wrong. Any participation in any virtue is a participation in the nature of God, and living the Christian life itself is a progressive *visio Dei*.[26] But let us go further.

For the monastic writers of the twelfth century, and for the regular canons as well,[27] the study of theology had as its goal not knowledge but salvation. They were, in fact, at one with the Venerable Bede, who defined theology thus: *Una ergo et sola est theologia, id est, contemplatio Dei*, "Theology, therefore, is one thing and one thing alone: the contemplation of God."[28] For Hugh of Saint-Victor, "study stimulates one's natural [mental] abilities, drives away idleness, engenders a love of knowledge, and preserves knowledge."[29] But more than this, study also "turns away the mind from vain and useless things, begets a hatred of sin, and seeks quietude and peace."[30] In other words, true study leads one away from *carnalitas*, and being led away from *carnalitas* is what *spiritualitas* is all about.

---

[25] See the brief and penetrating study by Odo Brooke, "Towards a Theory of Connatural Knowledge," *Cîteaux – Commentarii cistercienses* 18 (1967): 275–90, reprinted in Odo Brooke, *Studies in Monastic Theology*, CS 37 (Kalamazoo, MI: Cistercian Publications, 1980), 232–49.

[26] See Bell, *Image and Likeness*, 221.

[27] See Caroline W. Bynum, "The Spirituality of Regular Canons in the Twelfth Century," in Caroline W. Bynum, *Jesus as Mother: Studies in the Spirituality of the High Middle Ages* (Berkeley, Los Angeles, and London: University of California Press, 1984), 22–58; and Jean Leclercq, "Monastic and Scholastic Theology in the Reformers of the Fourteenth to the Sixteenth Century," in *From Cloister to Classroom: Monastic and Scholastic Approaches to Truth*, The Spirituality of Western Christendom III, ed. E. Rozanne Elder, CS 90 (Kalamazoo, MI: Cistercian Publications, 1986), 182.

[28] Bede, *In evangelium Lucae*, III.x; PL 92:471D: *Una ergo et sola est theologia, id est, contemplatio Dei, cui merito omnia justificationum merita, universa virtutum studia postponuntur.* Exactly the same definition appears in Bede's *Homilia LVII in die Assumptionis Mariae*; PL 94:421A, with *theoria* instead of *theologia*.

[29] Hugh of Saint-Victor, *De bestiis*, IV.xvii; PL 177:161C.

[30] Hugh of Saint-Victor, *De bestiis*, IV.xvii; PL 177:161C.

This happy situation was not to last. With the rise of the universities and the canonization of the scholastic method in the thirteenth century, the logical analysis of the faith was transformed from a means to an end, and by the fourteenth century much scholastic enquiry had degenerated into arid intellectualism, an impressive if useless display of rhetorical pyrotechnics. Spirituality had become separated from what we would now commonly refer to as systematic theology,[31] with great loss to both. Spirituality lost that essential solid theological basis without which it can degenerate into no more than warm and fuzzy feelings, and systematic theology lost the concept of connatural knowledge by which one knows not merely with the brain, but with the soul.

So what role does the direct unmediated mystical experience of God play in all this? It certainly represents the end of the path, its ultimate goal, and it is certainly of great interest to a great many people in the twenty-first century. There is a whole interconnected network of reasons for this, ranging from the discovery of the individual in the twelfth century to the interest in altered states of consciousness, drug-induced or otherwise, that is really a product of the twentieth. Those who would agree with William of Auvergne, that spirituality is simply that "by which we remove from our souls spiritual evils and seek to acquire for our souls spiritual goods,"[32] are, I suspect, a small minority. Far more people are interested in the highest reaches of the spiritual path such as we find described, for example, in the fourth degree of love in the *De diligendo Deo* of Bernard of Clairvaux or the fifth and sixth levels of contemplation in the *Benjamin Major* of Richard of Saint-Victor or, of course, the *Mystical Theology* of *ps.*-Dionysius.

---

[31] See François Vandenbroucke, "Le divorce entre théologie et mystique," *Nouvelle revue théologique* 82 (1950): 372–89.

[32] William of Auvergne, *De anima*, V.xii; *Guillelmi Alverni Opera Omnia*, II/ii:130. See Solignac, "L'apparation," 202, and "Spiritualité," 1145.

It is interesting here to compare the writings of the Carmelite John of the Cross, the friend of Teresa of Ávila, whom everybody knows, with the Dominican John of the Cross, whom nobody reads. The Carmelite John fascinates us with his meticulous discussions of the highest state and stages of the *via mystica* and the perils of the Dark Night of the Soul. The Dominican John maintains that spirituality has nothing to do with inner states and spiritual infusions, but that any Christian "who performs the tasks assigned to him with willingness and dedication is 'spiritual.'"[33] Furthermore, says Simon Tugwell,

> Over against the increasingly prevalent interiorism, Dominicans stressed that what matters is what one does, not what one feels like when doing it. It is going to Mass that expresses devotion, whether or not one feels inspired by it. Saying prayers, with a serious intention of addressing God, is real prayer, even if one's own mind wanders and even if one feels no devotion. In ways like this, the Dominicans tried to safeguard both the practicality and the integrity of the Christian life against the tendency towards a restrictive notion of what can count as spiritual.[34]

It is precisely this "restrictive notion" that, in general, dominates the discussion of spirituality today. It is the "squeamishness" mentioned by Robert Swanson,[35] and I wonder whether it accounts for the fact that in the invaluable and comprehensive *Dictionnaire de spiritualité* the Carmelite John of the Cross has a substantial entry devoted to him while the Dominican John of the Cross makes no appearance at all.

So where does Armand-Jean de Rancé stand in all this? He stands firmly in the tradition of *ps.*-Jerome, Guibert of Nogent,

---

[33] Simon Tugwell, "The Spirituality of the Dominicans," in Raitt, *Christian Spirituality II*, 29. John's works have been edited by V. Beltran de Heredia, M. Cano, D. Soto, *Juan de la Cruz: Tratados Espirituales* (Madrid: Ed. Católica, 1962). There is no English translation.

[34] Tugwell, "Spirituality of the Dominicans," 29–30.

[35] Swanson, *Catholic England*, 22.

William of Auvergne, and the Dominicans. In Rancé's France the term *spiritualité* had a multitude of meanings, some of them pejorative,[36] but for Rancé himself, *spirituality* could be defined as André Vauchez defined it for the Middle Ages: "the dynamic unity between the content of a faith and the way in which it is lived by historically determined human beings."[37] Rancé had read Teresa of Ávila[38] and had a profound veneration for Bernard of Clairvaux,[39] but nowhere does he dwell on their descriptions of ecstatic union with God. In his conference for the feast day of Saint Bernard, the Bernard whom Rancé sets before us is "Bernard the humble, Bernard the penitent, Bernard the follower of the Rule of Saint Benedict. He is not the Bernard of mystical rapture, not the Bernard of ecstatic experiences, something that Rancé actively discouraged."[40] He never denied that mystical experiences were possible—if he had, he would have been calling Saint Paul a liar[41]—but it was not a monk's business to solicit them. A monk's business was to live a religious life in community strictly in accordance with the prescriptions of the Rule of Saint Benedict and (in the words of the book of Tobit) "to bless the God of Heaven and bear witness to him in the sight of all who live."[42]

More than two centuries ago Charles Butler, an English Roman Catholic lawyer of enormous literary productivity,

---

[36] See Lucy Tinsley, *The French Expressions for Spirituality and Devotion: A Semantic Study* (Washington, DC: Catholic University of America Press, 1953), supplemented by Leclercq, "Spiritualitas," cited in n. 12 above.

[37] André Vauchez, trans. Colette Friedlander, *The Spirituality of the Medieval West: The Eighth to the Twelfth Century*, CS 145 (Kalamazoo, MI: Cistercian Publications, 1993), 9. This is a groundbreaking study. According to Principe, "Toward Defining Spirituality," 139, Vauchez here "seems to cast his net too wide." I cannot agree.

[38] See Bell, *Understanding Rancé*, 211.

[39] See Bell, *Understanding Rancé*, 133–36; Bell, *Saint in the Sun*, 147–84 (chap. 6), which offers a complete English translation of Rancé's conference on Bernard.

[40] Bell, *Saint in the Sun*, 154.

[41] See 2 Cor 12:2-4.

[42] Tob 12:6; see Bell, *Understanding Rancé*, 227.

published a biography of Rancé[43] in which he observed that prayer at la Trappe

> was both continual and fervent; but it never savoured of refinement, and, in all the agiography [*sic*] of La Trappe, a single instance of mystical excess, or even of mystical prayer, is not recorded.[44] . . . Far from endeavouring to penetrate the cloud with Moses, or to be admitted into the cellar of the Great King (such are the expressions of mystical writers), the monk of La Trappe aimed at no more, than to offer his prayer with the humble publican in the lowest part of the temple, or to fall, with the prodigal, at the feet of his offended but merciful father.[45]

Butler was quite right. There is no mysticism in any of Rancé's writings, no drop of water merging with wine, no drop of rain falling into a river, no two rays of sunlight uniting in one (this may be one of the many reasons that he is so little read), but there is certainly spirituality, and to the nature of that spirituality we must now turn our attention.

[43] See Bell, *Understanding Rancé*, 14–15.

[44] This is not quite the case. There are one or two very rare examples in the *Relations* of what Rancé would have described as the effect of extra-ordinary graces, but they do not affect the overall accuracy of Butler's statement.

[45] Charles Butler, *The Lives of Dom Armand-Jean Le Bouthillier de Rancé, Abbot Regular and Reformer of the Monastery of La Trappe; and of Thomas à Kempis, the Reputed Author of "The Imitation of Christ." With Some Account of the Principal Religious and Military Orders of the Roman Catholic Church* (London: Luke Hansard, 1814), 63–64.

Chapter Four

Rancé's Spirituality

Rancé's spirituality, like any spirituality, must be seen against its time and place. For the vast majority of people in Rancé's France, heaven and hell were real places, souls were real things (and riddled with sin), and God and the devil battled incessantly to claim them. Satan's business was to tempt the soul to vice, and he did so with great success; God's business was to lure the soul to virtue, and he had a much more difficult task. The demands of spirituality, therefore, seen as "removing from our souls spiritual evils and seeking to acquire for our souls spiritual goods,"[1] are not easy, and for Rancé and his colleagues they were made infinitely more difficult by their wholly pessimistic view of the nature of human beings.

At the root of this pessimism lay the idea put forth by Saint Augustine of Hippo that the entire human race was no more than "one lump of sin," *una massa peccati*.[2] Augustine's view

---

[1] William of Auvergne, *De anima*, V.xii; *Guillelmi Alverni Opera Omnia* (Paris: Denis Thierri, 1674; repr. Frankfurt am Main: Minerva, 1963), II/ii:130. See Aimé Solignac, "L'apparition du mot *spiritualitas* au Moyen Âge," *Bulletin du Cange, Archivum Latinitatis Medii Aevi* 44 (1985): 185–206, here 202; and Aimé Solignac, "Spiritualité," in *Dictionnaire de spiritualité* (Paris: Beauchesne, 1990), 14:1146–50, here 1145.

[2] See Augustine, *De div. quaest. ad Simplicianum* I, *quaest.* 2 *argumentum* and §16; PL 40:111, 121; and David N. Bell, *Understanding Rancé: The Spirituality of the Abbot of La Trappe in Context*, CS 205 (Kalamazoo, MI: Cistercian Publications, 2005), 75.

was that when Adam fell, the entire human race, which was potentially present in Adam, fell at the same time. We are the inheritors, therefore, not only of Adam's sin, but of his guilt. And not only that. Just as Adam's sin stained and corrupted his soul totally and completely, so our souls have inherited that total and complete corruption. We are not just sinful at birth, but one hundred percent sinful, and being one hundred percent sinful means that we cannot possibly do a single good action of our own accord. As Augustine says, "Of our own power we can only fall."[3]

Our only hope, therefore, lies in grace. But since we cannot do any good actions by our own power, we can never earn, deserve, or merit grace. God gives it freely to those whom he chooses, and the doctrine of predestination cannot be separated from the Augustinian doctrine of total human depravity. Some of us are predestined to receive God's grace; some of us are not. That is all there is to it. But since, in Augustine's view, we cannot know while we are still alive whether we are predestined to receive grace or not, we must act as if we were so predestined and do all that we can to please God.[4]

It is true that we are created in the image of God, but that image has been deformed by sin. And whereas the Orthodox East tended to emphasize the glory of the image (Orthodoxy accepts the doctrine of original sin, but has never accepted the doctrine of total human depravity), popular devotion in the West tended to emphasize the deformity. In the hugely popular twelfth-century *Meditationes piisimae de cognitione humanae conditionis,* "Most Pious Meditations for Understanding the Human Condition," incorrectly attributed to Bernard of Clairvaux, the inherent nobility of the soul serves only to contrast with the vileness of the flesh and the sinfulness of the body. We are sinners begotten of sinners and nourished in sin. We

---

[3] Augustine, *Enarr. in Ps.* 129.1; PL 37:1696.

[4] It must be understood that this is a simplified account of what is actually an extraordinarily complicated question.

are slime from slime, a fetid sperm, a bag of excrement, food for worms. We are ensnared by our senses, entangled in vice, itching for pleasure, possessed by passion, polluted by fantasies, and ever inclined to wickedness. We are conceived in sin, born in misery, live in pain, and die in agony.[5] "Why, then, do we so desire this life in which the longer we live the more we sin?"[6] Even more pessimistic, if that be possible, is the *De miseria humanae conditionis,* "On the Misery of the Human Condition," composed by Lotario dei Segni, who later became Pope Innocent III.[7]

These books were the best sellers of their day, and the inevitable result of this wholly pessimistic view of the human condition was to inculcate what André Vauchez and others have called a "penitential spirituality."[8] Such was the case in the Middle Ages, and such was the case in seventeenth-century France. Witness the view of Cardinal Pierre de Bérulle, founder of the Congregation of the Oratory of Jesus and Mary Immaculate, who died in 1629:

> The state to which we have been reduced by the sin of our first father is so deplorable that it has more need of tears than of words, more need of continual abasement of our soul before God than of any worldly speeches or thoughts that are too inconsequential to portray its reality. For in this condition, we possess the right only to nothingness and hell. We can do nothing but sin, and we are no more than a nothingness opposed to God, deserving of his anger and his everlasting wrath.[9]

---

[5] See Bell, *Understanding Rancé,* 77, for references to the *Meditationes.*

[6] *Ps.*-Bernard, *Med. piisim.,* ii.5; PL 184:488B.

[7] See Bell, *Understanding Rancé,* 77.

[8] See André Vauchez, *The Spirituality of the Medieval West: The Eighth to the Twelfth Century,* trans. Colette Friedlander, CS 145 (Kalamazoo, MI: Cistercian Publications, 1993), 139–40.

[9] *Œuvres complètes du cardinal de Bérulle: Œuvres de piété,* ed. Jacques-Paul Migne (Paris: Jacques-Paul Migne, 1856), 958, quoted in Bell, *Understanding Rancé,* 77–78.

This could have been written by Rancé. The language is not his, but the ideas certainly are. What can we do, then, but repent and do penance for our sinful condition and our incessant sinning? But more than that: in so doing we are doing no more and no less than imitating Christ himself. For Rancé and his contemporaries, Christ was the Great Penitent who lived his life and died an agonizing death doing penance for our sins. Here is Jean-Jacques Olier, the founder of the Sulpicians, who died in 1657:

> In honor of and in union with Jesus Christ Our Lord, penitent before God for my sins and for the sins of the whole world, I declare my intention to do penance all the days of my life, and to regard myself in all things as a poor and miserable sinner, an utterly unworthy penitent.[10]

Again, the words are not those of Rancé, but the ideas are unquestionably his. To say that Rancé's spirituality was a penitential spirituality, therefore, is simply to state the obvious. It is rather like saying that Rancé breathed. It could have been no other. But Rancé is careful to point out that penitential exercises for the sake of penitential exercises—asceticism for the sake of asceticism—get one nowhere. One of the problems here is that the French term *pénitence* may mean repentance, which is internal, or penance, which is external in the sense of *faire pénitence*, "doing penance." But if we start to take pride in the nature and number of our penitential exercises, they completely lose their effectiveness. It is rather like the Sufi story of the sheikh's beard.

There was once a Sufi teacher who had a long and luxurious beard. Each morning he would comb it and trim it until it looked perfect. But he found he was making no progress on the spiritual path. So one day, God (who is merciful and com-

---

[10] Jean-Jacques Olier, *Introduction à la vie et aux vertus chrétiennes: Pietas seminarii*, ed. François Amiot (Paris: Le Rameau, 1954), 23, quoted in Bell, *Understanding Rancé*, 89.

passionate) instructed one of his angels to visit the sheikh in a dream and tell him that the reason he was making no progress was his pride in his beard. When he awoke, the sheikh remembered the dream, realized its truth, and resolved that henceforth, every morning when he woke up, he would tear out half a dozen hairs of his beard until it was no more. Still he made no progress. Many days later, God, perceiving his efforts, had mercy on him again and instructed the angel to visit him again and again explain the reason for his lack of progress. What was the reason? His pride in pulling out his beard.

Rancé makes it clear that penitence is a means, not an end. Penitence, in fact,

> is no more than conforming our heart to that of God, and it demands the total sacrifice of ourselves. It does not consist only in weeping, but in weeping for what God wants us to weep.[11]

But how are we to conform ourselves to God, and how are we to know what he wants us to weep for? Rancé's answer is the answer of all the great spiritual guides: by overcoming our egocentricity and self-centeredness, and that, in turn, means eradicating our *amour propre* and *volonté propre*, our self-love and self-will. For Rancé, as a good Augustinian, will and love are essentially the same thing,[12] and the logic is then simple and straightforward. The less self-will/love we have, the more room there is for God's will/love. In theory, then, if we have no self-will/love at all, we may be a pure channel for the will/love of God. But there is a problem here. If we have no self-will/love at all, we shall die.

[11] Rancé, *Correspondance*, 1:560 (Letter 730611a), quoted in Bell, *Understanding Rancé*, 199.

[12] See Étienne Gilson, trans. L. E. M. Lynch, *The Christian Philosophy of Saint Augustine* (New York: Random House, 1967), 132–36.

Our bodies are like cars: they need fuel to operate. Our bodies do not, in general, need as much fuel as we push into them, but food is necessary if we are to stay alive. The commandment in the Hebrew Scriptures and the New Testament is not just to love our neighbors, but to love our neighbors as ourselves.[13] Putting it another way, a certain amount of self-love/will is required to keep us incarnate. A total and complete loss of self-will/love is possible only in moments of mystical ecstasy, when the soul is so united with God that there is no I left. But such moments, as all the mystics tell us, are brief and rare, and, as we saw in the last chapter, Rancé did not encourage them.

Long ago, Athenagoras of Athens, a second-century Greek theologian, said that the Spirit of God was one "who moved the mouths of the prophets like musical instruments."[14] One might be tempted to say, then, that our goal is to become a musical instrument on which God plays, having no will of our own. But the matter is more subtle than that. God's will, says Rancé, is done anyway, whether we like it or not. Even the demons do God's will, though they do it *malgré eux*, "despite themselves."[15] That is to say, they do not *want* to do it, but they have no choice. Our business is to cooperate with God's will, so that not only is his will done in and through us, but it is done with our consent and cooperation. Rancé is quite clear on this point:

> Jesus Christ says that his food is to do the will of his Father.[16] Our emptiness and aridity come from our not feeding on this food. This food never fails us, since we can never avoid doing the will of God. But it is not enough just to do his will: we must also wish to do it. Despite themselves, the demons do his will, but they do not want to. Everything obeys God naturally (*sans contrainte*). The whole of nature is obliged to

---

[13] Lev 19:18; Mark 12:31; and elsewhere.
[14] Athenagoras of Athens, *Legatio pro christianis* 7; PG 6:904C.
[15] See *Pensée* 257.
[16] John 4:34.

carry out his orders, and it is this that gives movement to all beings. Demons and sinners are the only ones who obey him despite themselves.[17]

In this case, it is not simply a musician playing on a violin, but it is a violin that is actually cooperating with the musician in performing and perfecting the music. It follows, then, that except in those moments of mystical absorption that Rancé does not promote, we must still have some self-will/love left so that we may stay alive "especially for the sake of fraternal charity,"[18] and become partners or co-operators with God in the work of creation. It is, in fact, a Jewish idea,[19] though Rancé could not have known that. In short, our goal is to eradicate, literally uproot, from our inner being those consequences of self-will/love that are truly selfish—primarily the seven deadly sins of lust, gluttony, greed, sloth, anger, envy, and pride—and place our self-will/love at the disposal of him who created it. Our goal is not to become mere automata, puppets in the hands of God, but rational human beings who have offered themselves to God and whose will, unlike that of the demons, is willingly to do his will. How is this to be achieved?

A key idea for Rancé (and, indeed, for a great many others) is detachment. There is a variety of French terms for this,[20] but the principle is the same for all, and it is the principle laid down in the first letter of Saint John: "Do not love the world or the things that are in the world. If anyone loves the world,

---

[17] *Pensées* 257–58.

[18] Thus Bernard of Clairvaux, Dil 10.27; SBOp 3:142. There are many things that call us back from that momentary (*ad momentum*) unmediated experience of God. There are the problems of everyday life, the ailments and needs of the body, but above and beyond all these, *fraterna caritas*.

[19] See Babylonian Talmud, Kiddushin 30b and Shabbath 10a. The Hebrew word is *shuttaf* "partner" or "cooperator."

[20] The most important ones are *détachement* "detachment," *dégagement* "disengagement," *dépouillement* "stripping," *désappropriation* "dispossession," and *desintéressement* "disinterestedness."

the love (*caritas*) of the Father is not in them. For all that is in the world is desire of the flesh and desire of the eyes and pride of life, which is not of the Father but of the world."[21] This does not mean that the things of this world are evil in themselves (that would be contrary to the statement in Genesis 1:31 that God saw everything he had made, and it was very good); the problem lies in our attachment to them. Detachment, therefore, does not necessarily mean the removal of physical objects or the elimination of relationships, but rather their taking second place to God and the things that pertain to God. It is stripping off the old self with its practices and clothing ourselves with the new self, "which is being renewed in knowledge according to the image of him who created us."[22] In the words of Henri-Marie Boudon, Grand Archdeacon of Évreux, who died in 1702,

> According to the apostle, stripping off [the old self] consists of renouncing worldly desires, that is to say, in detaching oneself from temporal, natural, and sensual things, in avoiding the riches of position, office, or marriage, and in forgoing all the pleasures that can satisfy the senses. These are the first steps that should be taken by the soul that truly yearns for God.[23]

They are also the first steps in restoring the lost likeness and in re-forming ourselves (as Saint Paul says) in the image of our Creator.

Detachment, however, involves detaching ourselves not only from the things of this world, but also from our own egocentricity and our own desires. It is detaching ourselves from ourselves so as to rely entirely on God. Not only do we strive to cooperate with him in doing his will, but we also accept

---

[21] 1 John 2:15-16.
[22] Col 3:9-10.
[23] See Bell, *Saint in the Sun*, 372.

whatever happens to us as being his will. Putting it another way, detaching ourselves from ourselves leads to a total and complete confidence or trust—the French word is *confiance*—in God. "All we need do," says Rancé, "is abandon ourselves to God, and when that is done, we have the right to hope for everything from his mercy. He foresees our needs and anticipates all our necessities."[24] By abandoning ourselves (*s'abandonner*) to God, Rancé means putting ourselves entirely in his hands. Once again, it is not a case of becoming a mere automaton or puppet controlled by God, but rather a matter of

> that giving of oneself to God in which one wishes to do his will whatever the situation and at the same time not only accepts the situation as the current context for this but actively wills it, as it were endorses it, since faith interprets it not as mere happening but as divine providence.[25]

In this condition, we accept all and everything that happens to us "with submission and holy indifference," and regard it all as coming from his hand.[26]

This is especially true of afflictions, sorrows, sickness, difficulties, problems, and pain. God sends us these things to test us, train us, and strengthen us with the intention that we should look "on everything we encounter on our path as coming to us by the disposition of Providence."[27] Afflictions are all part of God's plan, and the willing, even joyful,[28] acceptance of them is a clear indication of our total trust in God. Afflictions,

---

[24] *Pensée* 95.

[25] J. Neville Ward, "Abandon," in *A Dictionary of Christian Spirituality*, ed. Gordon S. Wakefield (London: SCM Press, 1983), 2. It is "the trusting acceptance of God's providence and the cooperation with him in obedience which together were seen as essential Christianity" (1). Ward's brief discussion cannot be bettered.

[26] *Pensée* 97.

[27] *Pensée* 92.

[28] See *Pensée* 139, and Bell, *Understanding Rancé*, 97–120 (chap. 5, *passim*).

says Rancé, "are the clearest indications we could possibly have of the care God takes in sanctifying us,"[29] and nowhere is this more evident than in the *Relations de la mort de quelques religieux de l'abbaye de la Trappe.* The most complete series was published in five volumes after Rancé's death,[30] and it cannot be said that they appeal much to our modern taste. The pages are filled with monks suffering from abscesses, ulcers, lesions, sores, fevers, tuberculosis, and a variety of other painful ailments (partly due, it might be added, to the inadequate diet at la Trappe), but triumphing over all these afflictions by accepting them willingly as the workings of divine Providence. The *Relations* make for grim reading, but they must be seen in the context of what in Rancé's France was the ideal of the "good death." At that time, says John McManners, "deathbeds were a place of polite resort and public ceremony."[31] Our ancestors, he continues,

> lived their lives on stage, and their concept of the family was broader than ours, bringing in more relatives, and servants and dependants. They died fulfilling and seen to be fulfilling their obligations to family and connection, their station and its duties.[32]

At la Trappe the family was the monastic community, headed by the Father Abbot, their station was their monastic profession, and their duties were those dictated by the Rule of Saint Benedict, the regulations of the monastery, and a willing acceptance of the will of God. A "good death" was therefore an edifying spectacle, which is why Rancé can say that "those

---

[29] *Pensée* 65.

[30] See Bell, *Understanding Rancé*, 257, for bibliographical details.

[31] John McManners, *Death and the Enlightenment: Changing Attitudes to Death among Christians and Unbelievers in Eighteenth-Century France* (London/New York: Clarendon Press, 1981), 234. See especially chap. 8, *passim*. This is a superb study.

[32] McManners, *Death and the Enlightenment*, 234.

who die either a good or a bad death often die more for [the benefit of] those they leave behind in the world than for themselves."[33]

These ideals of detachment, renunciation, loss of self-love/ will, complete trust in God and the ways of Providence, a holy indifference to afflictions or anything else that happens to us, and dying a good death all demand help. We cannot possibly achieve these things by our own strength, and, in any case, by our own power we can only fall.[34] Help, therefore, is essential, but whence does it come? It comes from three main sources: prayer, the Eucharist, and the nature, guidance, protection, and support of the monastic community and its superiors.

As to prayer, we are fortunate in having from Rancé's pen a considerable amount of information and advice on prayer and praying directed both to religious and to the devout laity. A detailed discussion is unnecessary since it has been offered elsewhere,[35] but the essence of what Rancé has to say may be summarized under four points.

First, it is better not to set down rules and regulations for prayer, but rather to leave it to the inspiration of the Holy Spirit. "We all have our own ways," he says, "and blessed are those who have no other [ways] than those that God has given."[36]

Second, to "pray without ceasing"—Paul's instruction in 1 Thessalonians 5:17—does not mean that internalizing of prayer described by many of the Eastern Fathers (and also by John Cassian), in which prayer continues uninterruptedly and forms a basis or substratum for all that we do, just as we can drive a car while enjoying a conversation with our passengers.

---

[33] *Pensée* 74.

[34] Augustine, *Enarr. in Ps.* 129.1; PL 37:1696.

[35] David N. Bell, "'A Holy Familiarity': Prayer and Praying According to Armand-Jean de Rancé," *Cistercian Studies Quarterly* 51 (2016): 343–72.

[36] Rancé, *Correspondance*, 3:66 (Letter 830508), quoted in Bell, "Holy Familiarity," 349.

For Rancé the instruction to pray unceasingly may be fulfilled by living the Christian life in general, and the monastic life in particular, with God as the beginning and end of all that we do. "We must never doubt," he writes to Madame de Guise, "that the most ordinary things we do, when done in this way, stand in place of a true prayer."[37]

Third, prayer may take any form, and the fact that one might not be able to attain its highest reaches is no excuse for not praying at all. Everyone can pray and, if they wish to be saved, everyone must pray, for, as Rancé says, "someone who does not pray does not have faith, which is the beginning of salvation."[38] But Rancé adds a note of caution. We must be very careful for what we pray. If we are going to ask God for something, we must examine the matter with the greatest care to be sure that what we are requesting is useful, appropriate, necessary, and in accordance with God's will. Prayer is as much listening as asking.

Fourth, prayer on its own is not enough. It must be joined with good works. On this matter, Rancé was at one with the writer of the Epistle of James, and he leaves us in no doubt on the question: "Prayers are of little use if they are not accompanied by the faithful performance of our works."[39]

Prayer, then, is "a holy familiarity, a sacred union of a human being with God."[40] It is a union of wills with God as the beginning and end of all our actions, and it is the key to salvation. "Prayer," says Rancé, "is no less necessary for preserving the life of the soul than breathing is for preserving the life of the body. Christians continue and make progress in the ways of God only in proportion to how much they pray."[41]

---

[37] See Bell, "Holy Familiarity," 365–66.
[38] See Bell, "Holy Familiarity," 365.
[39] *Pensée* 52. See also *Pensée* 75.
[40] Rancé, *De la sainteté*, 1:282, quoted in Bell, "Holy Familiarity," 345–46.
[41] *Pensée* 114.

As to the Eucharist,[42] it is a God-given channel of grace that, if approached worthily, can be "the remedy for all our ills."[43] Rancé has no time for those whose scruples lead them to receive communion but rarely. His view is that of Ambrose of Milan: "Receive every day what can benefit you every day; live in such a way that nothing you do may make you unworthy to receive it."[44] If the Christian life is the imitation of Christ, the Christ to be imitated is revealed in the sacrifice of the Eucharist. Baptism and penance are important, certainly, but they receive their power from the body and blood of Jesus Christ and the re-enactment of the Calvary sacrifice that is the essence of the Eucharist. In the Eucharist, where God is hidden under the species of bread and wine, you will find

the light of the blind, the strength of the weak, the healing of the sick, the comfort of the afflicted, and the refreshment of those who are burned by the fires of temptation. One can only be utterly astonished that we, who find ourselves in poverty, indigence, and misery, and who have among us this treasure of infinite value, do not have recourse to it and do not seek there the remedy for all the misfortunes that beset us and overwhelm us![45]

What, then, of the monastic community and the role it played in assisting a monk to achieve that detachment from *temporalia* and attachment to *eternalia* that is the very core of Rancé's spirituality? That demands a chapter to itself.

---

[42] For an examination of Rancé's views on the Eucharist, see David N. Bell, "Bread of Angels: Armand-Jean de Rancé on the Eucharist with a Translation of his Conference for the Feast of Corpus Christi," *Cistercian Studies Quarterly* 52 (2017): 277–309.

[43] Bell, "Bread of Angels," 309 (Conference §39).

[44] Ambrose of Milan, *De sac.*, V.iv.25; PL 16:452B, quoted by Rancé in §22 of his Conference for the Feast of Corpus Christi; Bell, "Bread of Angels," 303.

[45] Bell, "Bread of Angels," 302 (Conference §22).

Chapter Five

Rancé's Monasticism

All the important ideas we have seen in the last chapter—the role of repentance and penitence, the eradication of self-love and self-will, our cooperation with God in the work of creation, the need for detachment from the world, total trust in God and the ways of Providence, a holy indifference to afflictions and dying a good death—must be seen against the background of la Trappe. That is to say, Rancé's spirituality was not only a penitential spirituality; it was also a monastic penitential spirituality.

The logic here is obvious. The world is a dangerous place, and any interaction with it or the people in it is perilous. This idea appears again and again in Rancé's writings as well as in the *Pensées*: eight of them bear the subtitle "On the dangers of the world."[1] The things of this world are all transitory and changeable. They have no consistency or stability, and "it is a mistake and a terrible blindness to put the least value on things that appear for a moment and then disappear, and to neglect those that never pass away."[2] We must hold the world in contempt and scorn—the idea is stated in seven of the *Pensées*[3] and implied in others—not because it is evil in itself, but because our attachment to it is evil. There is nothing new in

---

[1] *Pensées* 60, 118, 129, 159, 160, 200, 226, 254.
[2] *Pensée* 149.
[3] *Pensées* 5, 11, 16, 58, 76, 149, 177.

this: it was the teaching of Saint John,[4] the Desert Fathers, and especially of Rancé's favorite, John Climacus, John of the Ladder.

Given, then, the grave danger of attaching ourselves to the passing allurements and temptations of the world, it is obviously safer to remove ourselves from it in the hope of diminishing its hold upon us. That is what the monastic life is all about, and a true monk, says Rancé, is one

> who has renounced the affairs, occupations, goods, honors, and pleasures of the world by a public statement, authorized by the Church, and has forever forbidden himself the use of them because of the contract he has made with God, who alone should be the object of all his thoughts, all his affections, and all his desires. This he should do in such a way that he can no longer make use even of those necessary things required by his human condition, save in reference to God and with the intention of pleasing him.[5]

It is true, of course, that the removal of temptations does not always stop one's being tempted. Our human imagination is as inventive as it is fecund when it comes to attaching ourselves to the *transitoria*. But it is also true that if one is not continually surrounded by tempting objects or situations, one is perhaps less likely to be tempted. The length of children's wish lists for Santa varies directly with the amount of advertising to which they are exposed. The world, however, is subtle, and Rancé knew it. "It is true that we leave the world," he says, "but the world does not stop following those who leave it, and the habits we have contracted there are destroyed only as a result of watching over what we do with the greatest care."[6]

---

[4] 1 John 2:15-16: see chap. 4, n. 21.

[5] Armand-Jean de Rancé, *De la sainteté et des devoirs de la vie monastique* (Paris: François Muguet, 1683), 1:2.

[6] *Pensée* 202.

In other words, entering a monastery will not solve our problems, but it may offer an environment in which those problems may be solved more effectively. That was the purpose of Rancé's monasticism.

Exactly what that monasticism involved is clearly set out in the two volumes of Rancé's *De la sainteté et des devoirs de la vie monastique*, first published in 1683.[7] The first volume is more theoretical, the second more practical, and must be supplemented by *Les Règlemens de l'abbaye de Notre-Dame de la Trappe, en forme de Constitutions*, first published in 1690.[8] Since I have provided a fairly detailed summary of *De la sainteté* elsewhere,[9] there is no need to repeat that here; but it will be useful, I think, to summarize the summary (and to add, here and there, a little more detail), for that will help us come to a better understanding of the content and teaching of the *Pensées*. The basic argument could hardly be simpler. Christ was the Great Penitent. The monastic life was instituted by Christ himself. The monastic life should therefore be animation of Christ the Great Penitent.

I doubt that many today would agree with the abbot that monasticism was instituted by Jesus Christ, and there were those in Rancé's own day who strongly objected to the idea. One of them was Daniel de Larroque, whose widely read *Les véritables motifs de la conversion de l'abbé de la Trappe* we discussed in chapter one. But Rancé himself was convinced of the matter. "Was it men who were the first founders and institutors of the monastic life?" he asks:

> No! It was Jesus Christ himself who founded it! And those whom he raised up to establish it in the world at the different times determined by his eternal foreknowledge were merely

[7] For bibliographical details, see David N. Bell, *Understanding Rancé: The Spirituality of the Abbot of La Trappe in Context*, CS 205 (Kalamazoo, MI: Cistercian Publications, 2005), 263–68.

[8] For bibliographical details, see Bell, *Understanding Rancé*, 275–76.

[9] See Bell, *Understanding Rancé*, 201–31.

the ministers who carried out his commands and the executors of his divine will.[10]

His dubious evidence for this comes from the gospels of Matthew and Luke, but the important point here is not whether the statement is true, but whether Rancé believed it to be true, and of that there is no doubt.

And what is a monk's principal duty?

> It is to dedicate himself to God in the tranquility and silence of his heart, to meditate unceasingly on his law, to keep himself perfectly detached from everything that might distract him from that end, and, by careful and continual application, to raise himself to that perfection to which he has been called by faithfully carrying out God's will and counsels.[11]

This is an admirable summary, and it at once leads Rancé into a discussion of the true meaning of poverty, chastity, and, above all, obedience. By obedience Rancé means absolute unquestioning obedience (he was attacked on this point by Daniel de Larroque), but it is not obedience for the sake of obedience. On the contrary. "Obedience alone triumphs over all the vices at once by destroying self-love and self-will, their source and foundation,"[12] and "the surest way [to spiritual advancement] and one in which we cannot be misled is to prefer in all things the will of our superiors to our own."[13] Rancé did not invent this idea: it is based solidly on the fifth chapter, *De oboedientia*, of the Rule of Saint Benedict.

Rancé then moves on to pose the question as to what God requires of those who are called to be monks. The answer is simple: they must love him. Indeed, without the love of God,

---

[10] Rancé, *De la sainteté*, 1:6. The last part echoes 1 Cor 4:1.

[11] Rancé, *De la sainteté*, 1:51.

[12] Rancé, *De la sainteté*, 1:101.

[13] *Pensée* 181.

withdrawal from the world is useless, and Rancé says so.[14] But although love is "an affection of the heart and a wholly interior disposition,"[15] it must express itself outwardly in what we do. Augustine, in a famous phrase, said *Dilige, et quod vis fac*, "Love, and do what you will,"[16] for if you truly love someone you will want to do all that you can to please them, and avoid all that you know displeases them. If this applies to humans, how much more does it apply to God? Rancé is insistent that inward dispositions must be reflected in outward actions, and at la Trappe these outward actions involved the meticulous observance of the regulations of the abbey. To try to avoid or mitigate the demands of the Rule is simply a result of self-love and self-will; obeying the Rule and one's superiors diminishes self-love and self-will, thus enabling us to know more of God's will and obey him more completely. For "chief among all the good things of this world is doing the will of God."[17]

Obedience to the Rule and one's superiors leads Rancé to a discussion of the place and responsibility of those superiors—and what a responsibility it is! Rancé, following Benedict,[18] sees the abbot as the representative of Christ in the monastery. As such, he must teach by both word and example, and his mission is not to impart doctrine but to instill piety. The key, once again, lies in a complete renunciation of the transitory and tempting things of the world, and an unswerving attachment to the things that last forever. And what is the essential reason for doing this? The answer again is simple: it is for the love of God.

The love of God, however, is but the first of the two great commandments, and the second is like it: "You shall love your neighbor as yourself."[19] Rancé therefore moves on to consider

---

[14] See *Pensée* 199.
[15] Rancé, *De la sainteté*, 1:133.
[16] Augustine, *In epistolam Johannis ad Parthos, tract.* VII.8; PL 35:2033.
[17] *Pensée* 140.
[18] *Regula S. Benedicti* 2.2.
[19] Lev 19:18; Mark 12:31.

the "fraternal charity," the *caritas fraternitatis* of the Rule of Saint Benedict.[20] Within the walls of a monastery and under a strict monastic rule, the number of ways in which one may show one's love for one's fellow monks must necessarily be limited. Particular friendships were strictly discouraged. Yet there are ways in which it can be done, not least (says Rancé), "by showing each other all those marks of gentleness, affection, and deference permitted by the rule of the monastery."[21] But of all these marks, the most important and the most useful is praying for each other. We saw in chapter four that prayer is as needful for the soul as breathing for the body,[22] but not only does prayer lead God to provide us with whatever graces we ourselves may need to persevere in his service; it is just as effective for those for whom we pray.

Prayer is the subject of the eleventh chapter of Rancé's *De la sainteté*, and I have presented a fairly detailed summary of its teaching elsewhere.[23] Prayer is the very cry of the heart, the inspiration of the Holy Spirit of love who opens our mouths and puts the words on our lips. Saint Benedict (says Rancé) demands that prayer be pure and fervent,[24] and "when we pray in community, he wants us to keep it short, for fear that because of the weakness and fickleness of the human spirit something should happen that takes away from the purity of so holy an activity."[25] Like everything else in monastic life, true prayer demands detachment from the things of this world and renunciation of our self-love and self-will. It must go hand in hand with our moral progress, and if there is no progress, that is a sure sign that one's prayer is not what it should be:

[20] *Regula S. Benedicti* 72.8.
[21] Rancé, *De la sainteté*, 1:246–47.
[22] See chap. 4, n. 41.
[23] See chap. 4, n. 35.
[24] Rancé, *De la sainteté*, 1:281, echoing *Regula S. Benedicti* 20.3-4.
[25] Rancé, *De la sainteté*, 1:281.

> If someone who prays does not become any better, and if he
> sees nothing in the faithfulness of his life that can assure him
> of the truth of his prayer, then he must believe that his prayer
> is no more than a delusion, the result of a duped imagina-
> tion.[26]

Prayer, like love, is obviously an interior disposition, but
"prayers are of little use if they are not accompanied by the
faithful performance of our works."[27] At la Trappe, the outward aspect of prayer was revealed in the faithful performance
of the penitential life, and Rancé now introduces a long chapter
on penance, penitence, and humiliations. There is no need to
say more on this than we have already said—Christ is the Great
Penitent, and the monastic life is the imitation of Christ—and
we have also seen how the idea of humiliations could easily be
misunderstood and how it led to a long and rancorous dispute
between Rancé and his one-time friend, Guillaume Le Roy,
commendatory abbot of Haute-Fontaine. The three chapters
that follow are devoted to meditation on death, to meditation
on the judgments of God, and, finally, to compunction.

Death is not only the necessary end of life, but a "good
death," something we discussed in the last chapter, was the
goal of a monk's existence. It was also, once again, an imitation
of Christ, who "died for our sins, in accordance with the Scriptures."[28] In advocating meditation on death, Rancé was simply
a man of his times. Today, in North America, Great Britain,
and much of Europe, we have sanitized death and removed it
from our immediate presence. In Rancé's France, death was
all around and eminently visible, and volumes like Jean
Crasset's *La douce et la sainte mort*—or, in England, Jeremy
Taylor's *Rule and Exercises of Holy Dying*—were the best-sellers
of their day.[29] A good death and subsequent entry into Paradise

---

[26] Rancé, *De la sainteté*, 1:291.
[27] *Pensée* 52.
[28] 1 Cor 15:3.
[29] See Bell, *Understanding Rancé*, 212–13.

were the goals and crowning achievements of the monastic life. It is never too soon to begin preparing ourselves for death,[30] says Rancé, not least because we never know when it may come upon us, and "a life of withdrawal is the true path to a peaceful death."[31] Meditating on death and the judgments of God expels sloth, cures inconstancy of soul, prevents the mind from wandering, makes penance pleasurable, destroys the bitterness of humiliations, kills intemperance, detaches us from earthly things, makes our prayers more fervent, inspires pious thoughts, and preserves devotion.[32]

The chapter on compunction, which ends the first volume of *De la sainteté*, is a mere eleven pages in length, and much of it consists of a series of quotations from a lengthy list of Desert Fathers and other patristic authorities. The theme is simple: weep for a few moments in this world so that you may live forever in joy in the next.[33] As Rancé says, "sins for which we have never wept continue to exist in the eyes of God: only tears can wash them away."[34] Yet again Rancé is a man of his times, for the seventeenth century was an age of public emotion, and tears flowed more freely, more openly, and more copiously than with most of us today.[35]

The eight chapters of the second volume of *De la sainteté* are more practical, and concerned more with the penitence of the body than the penitence of the spirit. There is much down-to-earth instruction here, and this second volume overlaps in a number of ways with the *Règlemens de l'abbaye de Notre-Dame de la Trappe, en forme de Constitutions*. Rancé begins with a very long discussion of withdrawal from the world, and then goes on to deal with silence, abstinence, and austerity in the monastic diet, manual labor, vigils, poverty (both interior and

---

[30] *Pensée* 174.
[31] *Pensée* 16. See also *Pensée* 136.
[32] See Bell, *Understanding Rancé*, 213.
[33] See Bell, *Understanding Rancé*, 214.
[34] *Pensée* 41.
[35] See Bell, *Understanding Rancé*, 88–89.

exterior), patience or forbearance in sickness, and mitigations, for which he has no time at all. The underlying themes throughout this second volume are total detachment from the world and the imitation of Christ as the Great Penitent.

In his discussion of withdrawal (*la retraite*), Rancé emphasizes the need for stability. That is to say, a monk should never leave or need to leave his monastery (which means that the monastery must provide everything he needs), and much of this lengthy chapter is devoted to showing that not one of the various reasons that a monk might propose for leaving the monastic enclosure, even for the briefest time, is in any way valid. Monks "are dead to all things of the senses. Their monasteries are their sepulchers, and that is where they remain at rest, waiting for the Savior of the World to call them forth as formerly he called forth Lazarus when he wished to bring him back from his tomb."[36] But what if one's parents were sick or indigent? Seventeenth-century France did not have Social Security, and aged and infirm parents of the poorer classes generally relied on their offspring to look after them. Surely this is a sound and charitable reason to leave the cloister?

No, says Rancé, it is not, but he is well aware that many in the world strongly disagreed with him. He therefore presents a long and detailed defense of his own viewpoint—it is obviously intended for his detractors, not for his own monks—and states unequivocally that the idea that the voice of the people is the voice of God is *not* one of the principles laid down in the Gospels.[37] He knows, of course, that his is the minority view, but "the greatest truths are those that have the least vogue and find the least approval among men and women, and the best precedents they can have is that they are either little known or much opposed."[38] Jesus Christ, he says elsewhere, opened one way and one way alone to lead his chosen people to Paradise, and what is that way? "It is the way of contradictions and

[36] Rancé, *De la sainteté*, 2:7.
[37] Rancé, *De la sainteté*, 2:136.
[38] Rancé, *De la sainteté*, 2:136.

the cross. Thus, the best and most profitable of worldly things are those that are most contrary to our inclinations."[39] In other words, the opposition, hostility, disagreement, antagonism, and just plain misunderstanding of what you do by those who belong to the world can be a sure sign that you are on the right path.

The absolute silence at la Trappe—the subject of Chapter XVII—fascinated the many visitors who came to the abbey. Rancé, following Saint Benedict, demands perpetual silence, and totally agrees with Benedict that if permission to speak is to be granted at all, it should be granted but rarely, "even to perfect disciples."[40] Otherwise a religious will easily learn how to say a very great deal in a very short time. Rancé sets forth as one of his best examples Saint Arsenius the Great, who guarded his silence so strictly that even the presence and authority of his bishop hardly sufficed to drag a word from his mouth. "When he was asked the reason for this, he replied that it was not possible for him to talk with God and people at the same time."[41] Rancé puts the matter in a nutshell in one of the *Pensées*:

> There is nothing that dries up the heart more or is more destructive to piety than useless conversations. Those who truly love conversing with God maintain a profound silence with human beings.[42]

Chapter XVIII deals with the thorny problem of the monastic diet demanded by the Strict Observance. This was a fundamental point of contention in the War of the Observances, and Rancé was well aware that the strict vegetarian diet at la Trappe was more demanding than that required by the Rule of Saint Benedict. He defends it, however, by adducing a multitude of authorities (something for which he was ridiculed

---

[39] *Pensée* 19.
[40] *Regula Sancti Benedicti* 6.3.
[41] Rancé, *De la sainteté*, 2:171–72.
[42] *Pensée* 183.

by Daniel de Larroque), and by pointing out that a purely vegetarian diet is an admirable example of penitence. Furthermore, he adds,

> If the regulations laid down by the saints for the edification of the Church, the maintenance of discipline, and the preservation of good morals produce the opposite effects, they no longer have any authority and they should not be heeded. There is no doubt that we should do away with the letter of the [monastic] rules when it is incompatible with the spirit. Do not think, my brothers, that this view is mine alone, for there were many great men and great saints who were of the same opinion.[43]

We now move on to manual labor, and "there is no penitential exercise, my brothers, that has been more practised or more recommended by monks than manual labor."[44] Its source is to be found in "the laboring life," *la vie laborieuse*, of Christ himself, but—alas!—"it has been abolished so generally that there is hardly any trace of it to be found even in the strictest observances."[45] This is to be regretted, for manual labor is a cure for idleness, a way of showing charity to the poor, an example of industry, and an exercise in humility.

"But would it not be more useful," asks Rancé, "for religious to employ their time in reading and study than in working?"[46] This leads us into the question of monastic studies that we discussed in chapter one, and, as we know, Rancé's answer is an unequivocal No:

> As we have already shown, monks were not destined for study, but for penitence. Their business is to weep, not to teach. And when God created solitaries in his church, his intention was to make not scholars but penitents.[47]

---

[43] Rancé, *De la sainteté*, 2:252.
[44] Rancé, *De la sainteté*, 2:257.
[45] Rancé, *De la sainteté*, 2:257.
[46] Rancé, *De la sainteté*, 2:292.
[47] Rancé, *De la sainteté*, 2:292.

The penitential life is continued by vigils, the subject of the brief Chapter XX. Not only (once again) is keeping watch at night an imitation of Christ, but sleep, according to ancient fathers, is "a real degradation, a condition in which the actions of the spirit are arrested, and while they are suspended we lose our human nobility and excellence and become just like the other animals over which God has given us such great advantages."[48] The time we are asleep is a dangerous time, for our imagination is filled with delusions, our minds with vain thoughts, and our memories with things that should not be remembered. To keep watch, on the other hand, "cools the heat of our lusts, as a great monk once said, banishes evil dreams, produces penitential tears, softens the heart, and makes us vigilant and exact in guarding our thoughts."[49] We must remember, however, that keeping watch is not merely a matter of forcing the body to stay awake and the eyes to be open. No. "It will be of no use to you," says Rancé, "to have your senses awake if your souls are languishing in drowsiness and sleep."[50]

The chapter on poverty that follows is long, but what Rancé says may be summarized under three headings. First, and most obviously, in poverty lies the imitation of Christ. Second, poverty must not only be exterior but interior. It must be a poverty of spirit as well as poverty of earthly goods (here Rancé, predictably, invokes Saint Bernard's criticisms of Cluny). There must be not just poverty, but a love of poverty, which is a different matter. And third, just as monks should be poor themselves, so they should do all that they can to assist those who are also poor. Here, as we might expect, Rancé quotes Matthew 25:32-46, that whatever we do or do not do for the least of our brothers and sisters we do or do not do for Christ. Hence the great importance of hospitality and almsgiving.

---

[48] Rancé, *De la sainteté*, 2:329–30.

[49] Rancé, *De la sainteté*, 2:331, quoting *le grand Solitaire* John Climacus, *Scala Paradisi*, XX.5; PG 88:910–11.

[50] Rancé, *De la sainteté*, 2:336.

Rancé's example of a poor man with a true love of poverty is Saint Bernard. "The love he has for poverty," he says, "flows into all his actions":

> this virtue lies in the depths of his heart like a living and abundant spring that pours forth its waters on every side. He is poor in all things and in all the places of his life. He is poor in his clothing, in his food, and in his belongings. He demonstrates it by his charity to the poor, by his unwillingness to acquire possessions or to undertake business affairs in order to increase the revenues of his community. In short, he testifies on every occasion to a perfect stripping off and entire lack of interest of all the goods, superfluities, intriguing things, and advantages of the world.[51]

Poverty and frugality, however, especially in matters of diet, are not normally the handmaids of good health. Nor were they at la Trappe. We have already seen that the startling mortality at the abbey caused adverse comment, and we have also seen that Rancé's logic was that of Saint Bernard and his ancient predecessors: a monk's business is to die with Christ, not to live with people of the world. If a monk falls sick, it is because God has intended him to fall sick,

> so that the pains caused by his affliction imitate that which Jesus Christ endured on the cross. Thus, by being more conformed to him, he may become more pure, more perfect, and more holy. He should therefore accept any sickness that happens to him not only with resignation, but also with thanksgiving, and should regard the pains that afflict him as remedies applied by God for the healing of his soul.[52]

Does this mean that sick monks should be left entirely to themselves and God and that no attempts should be made to

---

[51] Rancé, *De la sainteté*, 2:338.
[52] Rancé, *De la sainteté*, 2:431.

alleviate their sufferings? It does not. Remedies may be used provided they are cheap and common and provided they are recommended by the superior. A monk has no business asking for them himself. The remedies Rancé has in mind are primarily natural or herbal cures, the "roots, leaves, flowers, fruits, juices of plants, minerals, and other things found in the sea" mentioned by Basil the Great.[53]

Afflictions and pain, in other words, are sure signs of God's grace, and although this might not be the view of people in the world, it was certainly the view of Rancé. We mentioned this in chapter four and need say no more about it here.

There is no doubt that by Rancé's time, monasticism had lost its first fervor. Not all religious houses were in a condition of laxity or decadence, but many certainly were. According to Rancé, "this great Order of Saint Benedict fell into laxity from the second century after its foundation,"[54] and even the Carthusians, though they preserved their integrity longer than others, fell by the wayside.[55] Rancé's intention was to follow in the footsteps of Julien Paris and bring back *le premier esprit de de l'ordre de Cîteaux,* namely, the strict observance of the spirit of the Rule of Saint Benedict. That many would disagree with this was obvious, but as he himself said,

> If your way of life is neither approved nor appreciated by most people, you can take comfort from the fact that it has all the features and all the marks necessary to convince you that it is in accordance with the Spirit of God.[56]

---

[53] See Rancé, *De la sainteté,* 2:437, quoting Basil the Great, *Regulae fusius tractatae, quaest.* 55.2; PG 31:1046AB.

[54] Rancé, *De la sainteté,* 2:464.

[55] This was one of the statements that so irritated Dom Innocent Le Masson, General of the Carthusians. We discussed the matter in chap. 1.

[56] Rancé, *De la sainteté,* 2:495–96. See also *Pensée* 18: "When men and women disapprove of what we do, it is often the very mark and character of those things of which God approves."

It is only logical, therefore, that the very last chapter of *De la sainteté* should be a passionate and polemical attack on mitigations of every kind. We need not look at the details of Rancé's arguments: suffice it to say that in his view mitigations are "a violation of God's law, contempt for his instructions, a determined and wholly public resistance to his will, a ministry of wickedness, and, as a result, a state of death."[57] Some, it is true, may be lawful, but they are very few and are limited to those "established by the authority of the Sovereign Pontiffs and the constitutions of the Church."[58] These, and only these, may be embraced with a clear conscience, and they may be neither expanded nor modified.

Such, very briefly, are the main points of Rancé's monastic spirituality as we find it set forth in the pages of his *De la sainteté et des devoirs de la vie monastique.* How much of this may be seen in the *Pensées* selected by Jacques Marsollier? What has he included, and, more interestingly, what has he left out?

---

[57] Rancé, *De la sainteté*, 2:510–11.
[58] Rancé, *De la sainteté*, 2:527.

Chapter Six

The Spirituality of the *Pensées*

Given what Jacques Marsollier is trying to do, it is entirely understandable that certain aspects of Rancé's thought are absent. So what was Marsollier trying to do? He was trying to make Rancé more accessible to a wider public, to take his spirituality out of the cloister and make it applicable to anyone anywhere. Thus, if we look at the eight chapters that comprise the second and more practical portion of Rancé's *De la sainteté*, namely, withdrawal from the world, silence, the monastic diet, manual labor, vigils, poverty, patience in sickness, and mitigations, we see that half of them—the diet, manual labor, vigils, and mitigations—make no appearance in the *Pensées*. Nor, for the most part, is there any mention of the controversies that dominated so many years of Rancé's life. There is no reference to the clash between the two Observances, and there is no mention of the bitter conflict with Dom Innocent Le Masson. The long controversy with Dom Jean Mabillon on the question of monastic studies is relegated to a single *Pensée*,[1] and that with Guillaume Le Roy on the matter of humiliations to three.[2]

The question of silence is a matter for only two *Pensées*,[3] both of them concerned with the dangers of useless conversations, and there is but one sentence of immediate relevance:

[1] *Pensée* 207: see chap. 1, n. 27.
[2] *Pensées* 35, 36, 45.
[3] *Pensées* 183, 256.

"Those who truly love conversing with God maintain a profound silence with human beings."[4] Poverty, too, is the subject of only two *Pensées*. First, we are told that in order to pray well, "we must have poverty in our life and faithfulness in our conduct,"[5] but poverty here is poverty of spirit rather than material poverty. That is to say, detachment from the things of this world and, ideally, an absence of self-love and self-will. Second, in *Pensée* 234 on almsgiving, we are reminded of our duty to care for the poor, and Rancé echoes Matthew 25:31-46, that whatever we do for the poor, we do for Jesus Christ.

The matter of withdrawal from the world (*la retraite*), however, and patience in times of sickness and affliction are given much more consideration. So what does it mean to withdraw from the world? It does not necessarily mean entering a monastery, even though that might be the ideal: "Not everyone is obliged to follow the advice to leave the world [for a monastery], but the fact that we should have no love for the world is an indispensable obligation for every man and woman."[6] The word *monastery* does not appear anywhere in the *Pensées*, though three of them mention *the cloister* (*la cloître*), which can mean the same thing.[7] *Pensée* 180 tells us that if we seek in the cloister the peace and repose our souls desire, we must die to everything: not just to the dangerous world outside us, but to the dangerous world we carry in our hearts, "in the secret places of our soul." For unless we do this, "we will meet in the solitude just the same evils and just the same feelings we wished to avoid when we separated ourselves from human society."[8]

There are four other *Pensées* that mention a "solitude" where it almost certainly refers to a monastery,[9] and two that speak

---

[4] *Pensée* 183.
[5] *Pensée* 115.
[6] *Pensée* 94.
[7] *Pensées* 107, 130, 180. We shall consider numbers 107 and 130 in a moment.
[8] *Pensée* 180.
[9] *Pensées* 103, 178, 194, 232.

of *la vie religieuse*, "the religious life," which certainly means the monastic life. *Pensée* 13, a rich text, speaks of the essence of the religious life and the relationship between its inner spirit and external rules and practices, while *Pensée* 130 contrasts the immense difference between life in the cloister and life in the world. *Pensée* 107 is the only one that refers directly to *les religieux*, that is to say, "religious," or monks and nuns,[10] and it emphasizes their duty to be totally detached from the things of this world and totally attached to their Lord and Savior Jesus Christ: "Because God is their treasure, and it is he alone whom they should have in mind. All else is no more than an abyss of evils and misery."

What Marsollier implies, however, is that *la retraite*, "withdrawal," is not just for monks and nuns, but for everyone. It may be easier for those who have entered the solitude of the cloister, but (as we have seen) entering the cloister is not for everyone. It is the Johannine idea of being in the world, but not of it.[11] The *Pensées* speak of the happiness and sweetness of withdrawal,[12] pointing out that it is the path that leads to a peaceful death. Its essence lies not in cutting ourselves off from the world, but in cutting ourselves off from our attachment to the things of the world for the sake of the love of God. This last point is essential. Our love for God must be the sole motive for our withdrawal from the world; otherwise our withdrawal is useless. The more we detach ourselves from the world, the closer we come to God, and God, says Rancé, "will give himself to us in direct proportion to the faithfulness and care that we take in turning our face from the world."[13] *La retraite*, however, must be complete. If we separate ourselves from the world yet

---

[10] In French, the masculine plural *les religieux* may refer to male religious or to religious in general.

[11] John 15:19; 17:14-16.

[12] For reference to the various *Pensées*, see the index to the *Pensées* s.v. Withdrawal from the world.

[13] *Pensée* 109.

carry in our heart the remembrance of worldly things, we will be no better off than we were before.

Let us now turn to the matter of patience in times of sickness and affliction. A large number of *Pensées* are dedicated to this theme,[14] and we see here a reflection of Rancé's principle that the business of a monk is not to take care of his physical health, which is temporary, but to attend to his salvation, which is eternal. What the *Pensées* point out is that, first and foremost, our human suffering, whatever form it may take, is an imitation of the suffering Christ. "The cross is essential for Christians," says Rancé; "to live as a Christian is to live in suffering."[15] There is nothing new in this, and it has been the standard teaching of Christianity since the earliest times.

Second, accepting afflictions, sickness, and so on in peace and with patience strengthens our virtues and sanctifies our souls. But what is peace and what is patience? Both words appear in the *Pensées*—peace more than patience[16]—and for Rancé they mean much the same thing. By peace he does not mean the absence of war or the peace sought by the church when it prays *Da pacem, Domine, in diebus nostris,* "Give peace in our time, O Lord." He means rather an inner peace or quietude that comes from accepting whatever happens, good or bad, as the ways of Providence or the marks of God's mercy. This is what Rancé speaks of elsewhere as "holy indifference,"[17] and at its basis is our total submission to the will of God.

There are, however, two kinds of indifference. We might call them negative and positive indifference, though Rancé himself does not make this distinction. Negative indifference is when

---

[14] See the index to the *Pensées* s.v. Afflictions, Mortifications, Sickness, Sufferings, and Tribulations.

[15] *Pensée* 243. See also *Pensée* 19: there is but one way that leads to Paradise: the way of contradictions and the cross.

[16] See the index to the *Pensées* s.v. Patience and Peace.

[17] See *Pensées* 44 and 97.

something unpleasant happens to us that we cannot avoid and we simply shrug our shoulders and say "Whatever! Nothing I can do about it." Positive indifference is when something unpleasant happens to us that we cannot avoid and we take it as a form of instruction and teaching. First of all, we accept it as God's will. Second, since God's will always has a purpose, it must be something given to us for our profit, even if we cannot for the moment see it. And third, we should have no hesitation in asking God to help us understand his intentions for us, for "nothing happens to us, either inwardly or outwardly, that does not provide us with some occasion to perform acts of submission, charity, acquiescence, or patience."[18] If we may use a crude analogy, there is a difference between being caught in a heavy downpour while taking a walk in summer, and taking a shower. The end result may be the same—we get very wet—but there is a distinct difference in purpose. In other words, what Rancé means by "holy indifference" is that we do not just accept whatever happens to us because we have no choice, but we accept whatever happens to us willingly and, indeed, joyfully,[19] in the sure and certain knowledge that it is for our sanctification. This is what Rancé means when he says that "we must suffer in peace what we cannot avoid."[20]

Patience—the same word in both English and French—or forbearance mean much the same thing. When Rancé uses the word, he does not mean patiently waiting for something, but patiently enduring something. Yet once again, for Rancé *patience* is not just about enduring something, but how we endure it and our whole attitude to endurance. Simply putting up with (let us say) a toothache gets us nowhere. Trying to see the toothache as part of God's plan for us, and remembering

[18] *Pensée* 150.
[19] See *Pensée* 105. See further Bell, *Understanding Rancé*, 97–120 (chap. 5, "Rancé's Joy").
[20] *Pensée* 71.

that "we ought to suffer whatever afflictions God sends us in time not only with resignation but with joy, since we have reason to believe that this is to spare us in eternity,"[21] is an entirely different matter. I freely admit that when it comes to toothache I would need all the divine help I could possibly get to see the pain in this light, but nobody ever said that the spiritual path is easy.

Afflictions sent by God are a form of penance, though not a penance of our own choosing. On the other hand, as Rancé himself says, penances/*pénitences* sent by God are far more effective in bringing about the reconciliation of sinners than any penances we might choose for ourselves.[22] The word *pénitence*, in fact, is singularly lacking in the *Pensées*. It occurs but once in the plural, that we have just mentioned, and twice in the singular. That is in *Pensée* 41, where we are told that *pénitence*, which here certainly means repentance, demands tears. But though the word itself may be rare, the principle appears almost everywhere. Repentance—the *metanoia* of the Greek New Testament—is a change of mind, a change of heart, a change in outlook, a change in one's way of life. It is the *conversion*—the same word in both French and English—or change of direction from this world to the world to come, from *temporalia* to *spiritualia*, from the creature to the Creator.[23] In this sense, penitence is fundamental to Rancé's spirituality, for as we saw in chapter four, it is "no more than conforming our heart to that of God, and it demands the total sacrifice of ourselves."[24]

At the heart of Rancé's teaching on penitence, enduring afflictions in peace, patience, and holy indifference is submission to God's will, and here we come to the crux of the matter. Sometimes it is submission to God's will, sometimes (much

[21] *Pensée* 139.
[22] See *Pensée* 63.
[23] See chap. 2, n. 23.
[24] See chap. 4, n. 11.

more rarely) to the will of Jesus Christ, and sometimes to the ways of Providence.[25] Providence and the power of Providence were of first importance to Rancé and all seventeenth-century theologians. Providence is God's will in action and represents God's sovereign and beneficent control and direction of all that happens in creation. Whatever happens, therefore, is God's will, and to his will we are duty bound to submit. The prayer taught us by Christ himself says, "Your will be done on earth as in heaven." The principle of submission to God or to God's will appears again and again in the *Pensées*,[26] and, as Rancé says, "peace consists uniquely in the submission of our hearts to the commands of him who is their sovereign master."[27]

But submission to God's will is impossible so long as we are dominated by self-will. Here we are back with one of the essential principles of all spiritual teaching and one that we have had occasion to mention numerous times in earlier chapters, namely, the overcoming of the sense of self. For the Augustinian Rancé, self-will and self-love are the same thing, and—as we know—the less self-will/love we have, the more room there is for the will of God. But as we saw in chapter four, there is a difference between God's will being done, which is passive, and doing God's will willingly, which is active. Even the demons do God's will—God's will being what it is, they have no choice in the matter—but they do it *malgré eux*, "despite themselves."[28] The same is true of sinners: they, too, do God's will, though they would prefer not to.[29] In short, we cannot submit to God's will in an active, positive sense unless we know something of what that will is, and we cannot know what that will is so long as self-will prevents us from doing so.

[25] See the index to the *Pensées* s.v. Submission.
[26] See n. 25 above.
[27] *Pensée* 54. See also *Pensée* 70.
[28] *Pensée* 257; chap. 4, n. 17.
[29] *Pensée* 258.

The reason that self-will/love is so difficult to eradicate is our attachment to the world and the transitory things of the world. As we have said before, detachment from the world is essential, and there is nothing that receives greater emphasis in the *Pensées* than the dangers posed by the world.[30] The spirit of the world and the spirit of Christ have nothing in common,[31] and we are told of the folly of the world, the vanity of the world, and the nothingness (*néant*) of the world.[32] It deserves only our scorn, contempt, and hatred. The *Pensées* dwell on its fickle and transitory nature, its alluring temptations (especially for people of high rank and station), and particularly the insidious way that it will follow us when we try to leave it and will inveigle its way into our hearts: "The world is nothing but malice: it spreads it abroad everywhere, and, for the little time that we are here, it is very difficult to ward off its pernicious impact."[33] If we really and truly find no pleasure in the world, then we do not need to fear it,[34] but again and again Rancé hints at the subtlety of its attacks and temptations, and tells us that if we are like ships that continue to sail on the sea of the world, then "it is virtually impossible to avoid shipwreck."[35] And alas! Even if we leave the world altogether and withdraw to the safe haven of the cloister, unless we take the greatest care and pay the greatest attention to what we do, both inwardly and outwardly, even then "there are still times when it is possible to come to shipwreck there as in the midst of the sea."[36]

On the other hand, there are things to be learned in and from the world. "It is a great book that is forever open," says Rancé, "and people have only to read it to find therein impor-

---

[30] See the index to the *Pensées* s.v. World, the dangers of the world.
[31] *Pensée* 132, echoing Rom 8:1-17 and 1 Cor 2:12.
[32] See the index to the *Pensées* s.v. World, the.
[33] *Pensée* 119. See also *Pensée* 200.
[34] See *Pensée* 118.
[35] *Pensée* 159.
[36] *Pensée* 194.

tant lessons." The problem, he continues, is that those who learn these lessons do not apply them, and continue to regard all that happens in the world as "strokes of luck and not as the operations of Providence."[37] Yet the lessons remain, and being in the world and in the company of worldly people can have a good side as well as a bad. The bad side is obvious: the more we fill ourselves up with worldly people and things, the less room there is for God.[38] But the good side comes from the way in which what we are and what we do is regarded by worldly people. How so? Because the more opposition, antagonism, ridicule, and general misunderstanding we receive for what we do, the more likely it is that what we do is what God wants us to do. As Rancé says, "When men and women disapprove of what we do, it is often the very mark and character of those things of which God approves."[39] We saw earlier that the spirit of Jesus Christ and that of the world have nothing in common, for "the latter approves what the former condemns, and the latter scorns and rejects what the former seeks."[40] In other words, the more opposition we have from the world, the better we are for it.[41]

There are times, of course, when the world is going to win. With God's help (and only with God's help) we may overcome many of its temptations, but we will not overcome them all: "If we say we have no sin, we deceive ourselves, and the truth is not in us."[42] So what sort of a God is the God of the *Pensées*? Given the popular (mis)understanding of the abbot of la Trappe, we might expect him to be a savage and vindictive score-keeper, marking down every one of our many transgressions in a large book and smiling grimly when we fall into tempta-tion. Nothing could be further from the truth. He is a jealous

---

[37] *Pensée* 30.
[38] *Pensée* 226.
[39] *Pensée* 18.
[40] *Pensée* 132.
[41] See the index to the *Pensées* s.v. Conflict and opposition.
[42] 1 John 1:8.

God, that is true, which means that once he has chosen a soul and given that soul the grace to belong to him, he demands total loyalty and total devotion.[43] This is the God of the Pentateuch, who is a jealous God and a consuming fire,[44] but time after time in the *Pensées* Rancé emphasizes his mercy.[45]

Sometimes, to be sure, it may take both resignation and great faith to recognize his mercies, especially when they take the form of those afflictions he sends to test, try, and sanctify us, but God, says Rancé, "likes nothing better than to exercise his goodness on sinners. It pleases God to bring about great conversions,[46] just as it pleases a skillful physician to cure those who are desperately ill. And sometimes merely a trusting glance is enough to draw down upon us great mercy."[47] He is always there to help us in temptation,[48] and we would be foolish if we had the least hesitation in praying to him for his guidance and assistance. We saw in chapter four that prayer is as needful for the soul as breathing for the body.[49] Our love for God, says Rancé, engages his goodness, links us with his justice, and, in what may seem an odd phrase, "does holy violence to his mercy."[50] But doing holy violence—*fait une sainte violence*—is here an allusion to Matthew 11:12, in which Jesus tells the crowds who are there to hear him that the kingdom of heaven is carried off by violence. In other words, our love for God compels him to be merciful to us, if ever we may compel God to do anything at all.

On the other hand, as we saw in the last chapter, our love for God compels us to obey his commands and to do his will. We have to be strict with ourselves, and just as Rancé has no

---

[43] See *Pensée* 208.
[44] Deut 4:24.
[45] See the index to the *Pensées* s.v. Mercy.
[46] I.e., great changes in our way of life: see the note to *Pensée* 7.
[47] *Pensée* 12.
[48] See *Pensée* 222.
[49] See chap. 4, n. 41, quoting *Pensée* 114.
[50] *Pensée* 182.

time for mitigations within the monastery, neither has he any time for mitigations in the world. To give in to the world in even one tiny thing is to open a crack through which the world may pour in and overwhelm us, and we must continually watch over ourselves with the greatest care lest we relinquish eternity in the world to come for a few passing pleasures in the world we see around us. Thus, says Rancé, "there is nothing that induces God more to judge us with mercy than to judge ourselves with severity."[51] Yet when all is said and done, we may always find consolation in the straightforward and unequivocal statement that "the mercy of God knows no limits, and in all places as in all circumstances his omnipotent hand protects and sustains those who have the happiness to belong to him."[52] One cannot ask for more than that.

There is, however, another side to the matter. It is all very well for us to receive the gifts of God's mercy, but receiving the gifts of God's mercy puts certain demands on us. The Lord's Prayer does not just say "Forgive us our trespasses"; it says "Forgive us our trespasses *as we* forgive those who trespass against us." In other words, if we do not forgive, why should we be forgiven? For God to be merciful to us demands that we be merciful to others. "No one is ever without sin,[53] and if God puts up with us and our miseries, it is only just that we should bear with those of others."[54] And why does God put up with us and our miseries? The answer is simple: because despite all that we are and all that we have done he loves us, and here we come to the heart of the matter: God's love for us and our love for God.

Rancé regularly uses two words for love: *amour* and *charité*. In this he is following firmly in the footsteps of his patristic authorities who regularly distinguish between *amor* and *caritas*.

---

[51] *Pensée* 120.
[52] *Pensée* 197.
[53] See 1 John 1:8 quoted at n. 42 above.
[54] *Pensée* 141. See also *Pensée* 90 "On forgiving our enemies."

There is a third term, *dilectio*, that appears in both French and English as *dilection*, but this appears nowhere in the *Pensées*. It does appear in other writings of Rancé, but it is very rare. In the *Pensées*, *amour* and *charité* are almost equally distributed, and the difference between them is the difference we see in all the fathers of the church. *Amor/amour* is the general term, and may refer to any kind of love, good or bad, properly directed or misdirected, spiritual or carnal. *Caritas/charité* is love as it should be, and always refers to love that is properly directed. As Augustine said, "I call charity a movement of the soul towards the enjoyment of God for his own sake, and of oneself and one's neighbor for the sake of God."[55] Such is Rancé's usage. Charity is one of the three Theological Virtues (the other two being faith and hope), and Saint Paul provides a precise and exact description of its nature in 1 Corinthians 13:4-8.

That God loves us is not in doubt. The New Testament could not be clearer on this point. And his love for us is the reason that we love him. As Saint John said, "we love, because he first loved us,"[56] and we have already seen how our love for him "engages his goodness, links us with his justice, and does holy violence to his mercy."[57] God, says Rancé, "sets no limits on the love (*amour*) he has for us,"[58] and "we please God to the degree that we love him."[59] But loving God is not enough. As Jesus of Nazareth said, we must also love our neighbor.[60] Charity (*charité*), says Rancé, must be preserved at all times,[61] and that means that we must regard our neighbor in the best light possible. Perhaps the best summary of the duties and desire of charity is to be found in *Pensée* 91:

[55] Augustine, *De doctrina Christiana*, 3.16; PL 34:72.
[56] 1 John 4:19.
[57] See n. 50 above.
[58] *Pensée* 248.
[59] *Pensée* 252.
[60] Mark 12:31.
[61] *Pensée* 172.

> It is ever the duty of charity to regard all human intentions
> in the best light possible, and it is better to be wrong in
> believing something to be good when it is not than in letting
> ourselves believe something to be evil when it may well be
> that there is nothing evil there. The desire of charity is to
> avoid anything that can cause unpleasantness, and that we
> say only what can contribute to the calming and appeasing
> of the [human] spirit.[62]

In all that we have said above, there is nothing that requires
us to leave the world for the cloister. That may be the ideal,
but it is not a requirement. As we have seen, "Not everyone is
obliged to follow the advice to leave the world, but the fact
that we should have no love for the world is an indispensable
obligation for every man and woman."[63] Nor is there any call
for us to seek a path that leads to ecstatic self-transcendence
and mystical rapture. The spirituality of the *Pensées*, like
Rancé's own spirituality, is a spirituality without mysticism.
In the words of *ps.*-Jerome, it is simply "holding to what is
good and making progress therein."[64] The key is detachment
for the love of God, detachment from all created things so as
to be wholly attached to their Creator, and although this may
be more difficult to achieve in the world than in the cloister, it
remains an obligation. But let us never forget that in this we
are not on our own: God's love (says Rancé) is infinite, his
mercy knows no limits, and he is always eager to respond to
the prayers of those who belong to him.

The *Pensées*, therefore, represent what we might call "Rancé
for all," but they are not designed for consecutive reading.
They do not offer us a systematic and logical presentation of
Rancé's monastic spirituality—that may be found in the two
volumes of *De la sainteté*—but they do, in my view, help us

---

[62] See also *Pensée* 195 on judging our neighbor favorably.
[63] See n. 6 above.
[64] See chap. 3, n. 14.

penetrate to the heart of that spirituality and take it out of the cloister. Rancé's friends compared the *Pensées* to the *Pensées* of Blaise Pascal,[65] but the two collections are very different. Pascal is trying to present an *apologia* for Christianity; Rancé, in the hands of Jacques Marsollier, is trying to provide us with a concise unmystical map of the highway that leads to heaven. Rancé's *Pensées* are more similar to the sayings of the Desert Fathers, with which, indeed, they have much in common, and are best dipped into rather than read. In translating them, I found that one *Pensée* would have a far deeper impact than another. Some I did not like at all, but (as Rancé says) those were sometimes the ones I needed most to absorb. When reading through the translation after I had completed it, it was a different set of *Pensées* that had their impact. Translating brief passages out of their context can sometimes be tricky, though in only two cases—*Pensées* 156 (the first sentence) and 211—am I really uncertain as to what Rancé is saying. What follows, then, is the first English translation of Rancé's thoughts and reflections, and if it does not please the reader, then I can only beg him or her to be charitable and remember Rancé's advice in *Pensée* 236:

> We never express our opinions with too much vehemence and enthusiasm. It is better to be prudent and yield than to prevail at the expense of charity.

---

[65] See chap. 2, n. 7.

Part Two

The Translation

Abbreviations

M: Marsollier: The text of the *Pensées* as it appears in both
      editions of Jacques Marsollier: *La vie de Dom Armand-*
      Jean de Bouthillier de Rancé, abbé régulier et réformateur du
      Monastère de la Trappe. 1st ed. Paris: Jean de Nully, 1703.
      3–83 of the separately paginated appendix. 2nd ed.
      Nouvelle Édition. Paris: Chez Savoye, 1758. 501–75.

M¹: The text of the *Pensées* as it appears in the first edition
      only (1703) of Jacques Marsollier's *La vie de Dom*
      Armand-Jean de Bouthillier de Rancé.

M²: The text of the *Pensées* as it appears in the second edi-
      tion only (1758) of Jacques Marsollier's *La vie de Dom*
      Armand-Jean de Bouthillier de Rancé.

P: *Pensées et réflexions de M. de Rancé, Abbé de la Trappe.*
      Paris: Chez Vente, 1767.

The Three Editions
and the Translation

M^2 is a fairly faithful copy of M^1, with the headings of the
Pensées being moved from the top of the *Pensées* to the margin.
A comparison of the two editions reveals about forty variants,
of which only a handful are of any significance. These are noted
in the footnotes to the translation. The other variants include
changes from singular to plural, a few changes in the tenses
of verbs, some word inversions (e.g. *une éternelle obligation/
une obligation éternelle*), and minor grammatical amendments.
Other than these, the main difference between M^1 and M^2 lies
in the punctuation, which, in general, is much better and much
clearer in M^2 than in M^1.

P has been subjected to much more comprehensive editing
than M^2, and there is a very large number of variants. The
punctuation, too, has been further amended. Once again, most
of the variants make no difference to the translation: those that
do (or might) are noted in the footnotes. What is more important is that if Marsollier has attempted to make Rancé accessible to a wider public than enclosed religious, the editor of P
has tried to appeal to an even broader audience. For example,
the untranslated Latin tags that appear in *Pensées* 185, 187, and
240 are tacitly omitted in P. The strong "always, always" in
Pensée 22—"Good things are always to be feared, since they
are always able to harm us"—is softened to "often to be feared"
and "often able to harm us." A similar amendment is to be seen
in *Pensée* 20, where P adds "very often" to tone down the harsh-
ness of the text in M. Sometimes, however, P is stronger then

M, as in *Pensée* 99: it is not that we *should* subject ourselves to God, we *must* subject ourselves to God. In *Pensée* 10 the entire audience has been changed from high-ranking ecclesiastics to everyone, though it must be admitted that the change does not really work. Nor does it work in *Pensée* 28, where the editor has changed "the dangers of good works," which is accurate, to "the usefulness of recollection," which is not. And there are a number of cases when words have been altered to make the sense of the *Pensée* clearer. All significant variants are noted in the footnotes, but those that make no difference at all to the translation are not. This is not a critical edition of the French text.

As we saw at the end of Chapter Two, the version that appears in the *Histoire de l'abbé de Rancé* of Philippe-Irenée Boistel d'Exauvillez rearranges the *Pensées* according to subject matter, but makes no other contribution either to the text or to the present translation.

The translation is based on the text in P, though that must sometimes be amended from M. The enumeration of the *Pensées* is also that which appears in P, since the numbering in both M^1 and M^2 is faulty. The numbering in all three editions is in Roman numerals, but since these can become cumbersome, I have added Arabic numbers in parentheses to make life easier. All biblical citations have been translated from the Vulgate text, and the enumeration of the Psalms is also that of the Vulgate. All translations are my own.

It is always tempting with a work such as this to add to each *Pensée* a note explaining what Rancé is saying or seems to be saying. Except in a very few instances, where the content of the *Pensée* is obscure or where I am by no means certain as to what Rancé means, I have not succumbed to the temptation. Had I done so, the result would have been the Thoughts and Reflections of David N. Bell, which are certainly not worth pondering, rather than the Thoughts and Reflections of Armand-Jean de Rancé, abbot of la Trappe, which are.

Thoughts and Reflections on Various Subjects of Piety[1]

I (1)

On the good use of graces

There is no better way to persuade God never to withdraw from us those graces with which he has begun to favor us than to take the greatest care to put them to good use.[2]

II (2)

On consulting God in everything

We should never undertake anything unless we are absolutely sure[3] that God calls us to do it; for it often happens that we let ourselves be seduced by gleams of good things that present themselves to us, and—following our own desires and not the commandment of God—our goals have neither the effect nor the success we had in mind. The only thing we feel is sorrow for having been involved at all.

---

[1] This is the title in P. The title in M (both editions) is *Thoughts of the Abbot of la Trappe on Various Subjects of Piety, Taken from his Spiritual Letters.*

[2] Throughout the *Pensées*, Rancé is insistent that our knowledge, faith, belief, confidence, or anything similar, must be manifested in practical outward activities. In other words, as the Epistle of James makes clear, faith must go hand in hand with good works. See *Pensées* 42, 52, 56, 75, 101, 158, 169, and 227.

[3] M: *qu'il ne nous soit evident que Dieu*; P: *que nous n'ayions toute la certitude possible que Dieu*. P makes the phrase stronger.

III (3)

That we should be attached only to God

The changeability of things here below should make it clear to us that only God is unchangeable, that he remains ever the same, that we can never lose him, provided we wish to keep him, and that he deserves to be the sole object to which our hearts are attached.

IV (4)

On the horror of sin

There is but one thing in this world that should bring us grief and cause us sorrow, and that is sin. But when our life is freed from [sin], then, whatever may happen, we will remain at peace,[4] for if God is content, so should we be, since his will alone should rule ours.

V (5)

On hating the world and loving eternity

If we want to make as strong a case for eternity as it deserves, we must begin by hating the world and holding it in contempt, for what is certain is that to the same degree that the world diminishes in our heart, so eternity increases and takes over all the places and empty spaces [the world] has left behind.

VI (6)

On fleeing positions of importance,
and trusting in God when he calls us to them

When we take no steps and make no effort to find ourselves important positions,[5] there is reason to believe that God will

---

[4] What Rancé means by peace/*paix* is discussed in chap. 6.

[5] The text simply has *les emplois* "posts, occupations," but the subtitle has *grandeurs*, which implies positions of rank, greatness, and importance.

not refuse us the protection he normally gives to those who follow the orders of his Providence,[6] and who regard these things from a Christian point of view.[7] They see these things as coming from his hand, although they are conveyed by the hands of ordinary people.

VII (7)

On the danger of delaying our changing our way of life[8]

It is to be feared that while we prevaricate about changing our way of life and remain undecided, our will may weakened by keeping up our interaction with the world, and our old, ingrained habits may destroy our intentions, which are still fragile and have only just been brought to birth.

---

[6] The importance of Providence has been mentioned in chap. 6. Providence is God's will in action and represents God's sovereign and beneficent control and direction of all that happens in creation. We must note, however, that human beings are not mere puppets in the hands of Providence, but willing co-workers with God in the work of creation, though in this cooperation, God's work is always primary and ours is always secondary. Furthermore, this cooperation is possible only through God's grace, for without that grace we are nothing. In short, if we willingly subject ourselves to the movement of God's Providence—if we willingly follow its orders—God's Providence will look after us. See further David N. Bell, *A Saint in the Sun: Praising Saint Bernard in the France of Louis XIV*, Cistercian Studies Series 221 (Collegeville, MN: Cistercian Publications, 2017), 545, s.v. "Providence."

[7] See Matt 6:25-34: if God looks after the flowers of the field and the birds of the air, will he not look after us?

[8] "Changing our way of life" represents Rancé's term *conversion*, on which see chap. 2, n. 23. The essence of conversion is detaching ourselves from the transitory things of this world and attaching ourselves to the unchangeable things that pertain to eternity. "Detachment" is one of the main themes of the *Pensées*, as, indeed, it is one of the main themes of the whole of Rancé's writings. See further Bell, *Saint in the Sun*, 542–43, s.v. "*Dégagement*/detachment."

VIII (8)

That patience⁹ should be joined with suffering

It is not enough to suffer in patience if our patience is not persevering, and if it does not have the steadfastness and scope needed to resist not only the violent attacks of evils, but the tedium¹⁰ that is almost inseparable from them when they go on for any length of time.

IX (9)

On the benefits of the mortifications that God sends us

The afflictions that are sent us from God are the most common and most effective means he uses to cut out from us what can displease him and restore us entirely to what his heart desires.

---

⁹ What Rancé means by *patience*—patience or forbearance—has been discussed in chap. 6.

¹⁰ *Ennui*, which may mean no more than worry or anxiety, but which usually means something far more serious, namely, that *acedia*/accidie so deeply feared by so many early monastic writers. Evagrius of Pontus regarded the demon of accidie as the most dangerous of all demons, John Cassian presents a long and brilliant account of accidie and its perils in Book 10 of his *Institutes*, and Thomas Aquinas examines it with his usual lucidity in the *Summa theologica, Secenda secundae, quaestio* 35. According to Cassian, accidie brings about a dislike of one's monastery, disgust with one's cell, an inability to focus on anything, a preoccupation with one's health and well-being, an inappropriate interest in one's food and meals, an unsettled state of mind and spirit, and boredom with whatever one is doing or has to do. And besides this, a monk in the grip of accidie "looks about anxiously this way and that, and sighs that none of the brothers happen to come by. He often wanders in and out of his cell and gazes up at the sun as if it were taking too long to set. And in this way he is filled with a sort of irrational confusion of mind, like an earthly darkness, and becomes indifferent and useless (*otiosus et vacuus*) for any kind of spiritual work" (John Cassian, *De coenobiorum institutis*, 10.2; PL 49:367B). It is not, of course, restricted to monks and nuns. Accidie/*ennui* lurks in ambush for anyone who is seriously trying to follow a spiritual path. After the first positive impetus our initial enthusiasm always fades, and there inevitably follows a period of intense, unforgiving, and unrewarding boredom.

X (10)
On duties made easy[11]

The way to not be overwhelmed by the burden of our duties is to be afraid of being overwhelmed; for generally speaking, we avoid precipices when we have a dread of falling over them.

XI (11)
That Christians should hold earthly things in contempt

Earthly things, however alluring they may be, ought not to occupy Christians for a single moment. They should live in the faith, anticipation,[12] and vision of those things that are eternal.

XII (12)
That great sinners should trust in God

Whoever has sinned can take comfort in the fact that God likes nothing better than to exercise his goodness on sinners.[13] It pleases God to bring about great conversions,[14] just as it pleases

---

[11] By changing just a few words, P changes entirely the nature of this saying and the scope of its audience. Marsollier's subtitle is "On the dangers of high rank in the Church (*dignités ecclésiastiques*)," which applies, by definition, to high-ranking ecclesiastics. P has "On duties made easy," which applies to everyone. For M's *la pesanteur des charges ecclésiastiques* ("the weight of ecclesiastical responsibilities"), P substitutes *le poids de ses devoirs* "the burden of one's duties." It must be admitted, however, that the version in P does not really work. The advice is certainly useful for anyone who has been invited to take up a high position in the church or, indeed, in any other organization. Think carefully about what it involves and what it demands, and then make a decision. It is not really applicable to those of us who are simply trying to fulfill our Christian duties. Indeed, it might easily dissuade us from undertaking them at all.

[12] I.e. of the Second Coming of Christ. See *Pensée* 259.

[13] M[1]: *sur les grands pécheurs* "on great sinners"; M[2]: *sur les plus grands pécheurs* "on the greatest sinners"; P: *sur les pécheurs* "on sinners." There is no contradiction. If God is happy to forgive *les plus grands pécheurs*, we may assume that he is also happy to forgive the common or garden variety, like us.

[14] I.e. great changes in our way of life: see the note to *Pensée* 7.

a skillful physician to cure those who are desperately ill. And sometimes merely a trusting glance is enough to draw down upon us great mercy.

XIII (13)

On the duties of the religious life

The religious life is [to be found] entirely in the spirit, and even though all the external rules and practices are necessary, they are[15] no more than the means to acquire that detachment[16] and purity of heart[17] that comprise the whole essence of the religious life.

XIV (14)

On the benefits of being disgraced[18]

We should never regard being disgraced as blows of misfortune, but rather as the purposes and guidance of the mercy of

---

[15] M adds *néanmoins* "nevertheless."

[16] *Détachement*: see note to *Pensée 7* and n. 17 below.

[17] For the Desert Fathers and John Cassian (Rancé was intimately acquainted with all of them), and for a host of other writers, complete detachment and purity of heart/*puritas cordis* are essentially the same thing. Only a heart that is perfectly detached from earthly things is sufficiently pure to see God (see Matt 5:8), and perfect detachment from earthly things demands the complete abolition of self-love and self-will. In Cassian, *puritas cordis* is his Latin translation of the Greek *apatheia*, the goal of the Byzantine spiritual tradition. *Apatheia* has nothing whatever to do with the English term *apathy*. It is rather the restoration of the lost likeness and the realization of our potential in being created *ad imaginem Dei*: see further David N. Bell, "*Apatheia*: the Convergence of Byzantine and Cistercian Spirituality," *Cîteaux – Commentarii cistercienses* 38 (1987): 141–64.

[18] In this *Pensée, la Cour* can only mean the Royal Court, and that, if we are to be literal, is somewhat limiting. Few of us are courtiers, and fewer still courtiers under so capricious a monarch as Louis XIV. Those who frequented the halls of Versailles were very careful about what they did, what they said, and to whom they said it. On the other hand, to be taken down a peg (to use the English expression) probably does us no harm, although—speaking personally—we might find it extremely disagreeable.

God. He makes use of unforeseen events to lead those whom he loves,[19] by a special protection, from the midst of the [royal] Court as from the midst of a shipwreck.

XV (15)

That mortifications are useful

The mortifications that God sends us are much more effective [in guiding us] to eternity than those we can choose for ourselves.

XVI (16)

On the benefits of withdrawal [from the world][20]

A life of withdrawal is the true path to a peaceful death,[21] and to die in the love and joy of eternal things, we must have lived in contempt and hatred of those that are temporal.

XVII (17)

That we cannot rely on the things of this world

What do people think? Everything slips away in this world with tremendous speed: at every moment we are poised to lose what we truly love. Yet we treat eternity like time, and time, by a deplorable inversion, holds in our hearts the place that eternity alone should[22] occupy.

---

[19] M: *ceux qu'il aime* "those whom he loves"; P: *l'homme de bien*, which could mean either an upright man or a man of property.

[20] *La retraite*. We discussed this at some length in chap. 6.

[21] Armand-Jean de Rancé, *De la sainteté et des devoirs de la vie monastique* (Paris: François Muguet, 1683), 2:30: "If, in the order of God, all Christians live only to die, and if the whole of their lives should be simply a preparation for death, how much more should this be true of a monk?" *De la sainteté* 2:459: "Solitaries, as we have said so many times, do not come to monasteries to live there, but to die there." See further chap. 1, nn. 17–19.

[22] M: *devroit* (present conditional); P: *doit* (present indicative).

XVIII (18)

On consulting God in good works

When men and women disapprove of what we do, it is often the very mark and character of those things of which God approves.[23]

XIX (19)

On the necessity of sufferings

Jesus Christ opened but one way to lead all people to the bliss he intended for them: it is the way of contradictions and the cross. Thus, the best and most profitable of worldly things are those that are most contrary to our inclinations.

XX (20)

That God uses the unjust actions of
men and women to our advantage

The unjust actions of men and women are very often[24] the just actions of God, who uses them, contrary to their intentions, to our advantage.

XXI (21)

On abstaining from what is good in order to please God

There are times when, for holy reasons, we must abstain from things that are good in themselves.

XXII (22)

On offering[25] *everything to God*

To belong to God, we must put the good and bad things of this world to the test. Good things are often to be feared, since they

---

[23] See also Rancé, *De la sainteté*, 2:136, quoted in chap. 5, n. 38.

[24] M omits "very often" (*très-souvent*).

[25] Lit. "sacrificing" (*sacrifier*).

are often able to harm us;[26] bad things are always useful for us, provided we make use of them in a holy way.

XXIII (23)
On willing only God

To enjoy God to the full, we must be wholly detached[27] from all transitory things;[28] for he gives himself to us only to the extent that we give ourselves to him.

XXIV (24)
On suffering in patience

There is more to be gained in suffering evils we cannot prevent than in doing what we believe to be, and what appear to be, great works.

XXV (25)
On submission to God

God takes pleasure in thwarting our best and most holy intentions. What they are worth before God is not determined by their success: all he asks of us[29] is submission to his will.

---

[26] M has "Good things are always (*toujours*) to be feared, since they are always (*toujours*) able to harm us." P softens this to *souvent . . . souvent* "often . . . often."

[27] Lit. "we must be in a total *désoccupation*," which means being totally unoccupied with, separated from, detached from earthly things. *Désoccupation* may be regarded as a synonym for *détachement* and *dégagement*: see nn. 8 and 17 above.

[28] M: *de tout ce qui passe*; P: *de tout ce qui se passe*.

[29] P omits "of us" (*de nous*).

XXVI (26)

That our goal[30] *should be God alone*[31]

When we have in view any other end but God, all we find are tribulations and disquiet.

XXVII (27)

On our love for God[32]

Even though God may move in such a way as to convince us of the obligation we have to dissociate[33] ourselves from the love and attachment we have for the world, we live in it as if we should never leave it.

XXVIII (28)

On the usefulness of recollection[34]

Self-love is often to be found in actions that seem to us to be the best possible, and it is difficult to be certain of the purity of our intentions. The life of withdrawal [from the world] safeguards us from all these drawbacks.

---

[30] *Fin*: "goal, end, purpose, destination, aim, object." In other words, God should be in our mind, our vision, and our thoughts in everything we do, and all that we do should be in accordance with his intentions.

[31] The subtitle in M is simply *Dieu seul*, "God alone." P expands this to *Dieu seul notre fin*. *Dieu seul* was an expression especially associated with Henri-Marie Boudon, grand archdeacon of Évreux, and it caused some controversy in the second half of the seventeenth century. Boudon's *Dieu seul, ou l'association pour l'interêt de Dieu seul* was published in 1662 and placed on the Index in 1688 because of its Quietist tendencies. See Bell, *Saint in the Sun*, 356–57. By the time of Marsollier's biography, however, the controversy was largely forgotten.

[32] For *Amour de Dieu* in P, M has *Amour du monde* "On our love for the world," which is more accurate and a better subtitle.

[33] *Se dégager*: "to extricate oneself, free oneself, break loose from, disengage oneself, disassociate oneself, escape from."

[34] *Recueillement* or recollection is an important technical term in seventeenth-century French spirituality and is discussed in Bell, *Saint in the Sun*, 545–46.

XXIX (29)

On submission to the will of God

The best or, rather, the only course we should take in the things that happen to us in our lives, whether they be of lesser or greater importance, is to have only God before our eyes, to conduct ourselves with a view to pleasing him, and, in all things, to act in accordance with his intentions.

XXX (30)

That we profit little from the lessons the world teaches us

The world is a great book that is forever open, and people have only to read it to find therein important lessons. Unfortunately, [these lessons] are never applied, and the things that happen in the world are regarded as strokes of luck and not as the operations of Providence.[35]

XXXI (31)

On the benefits of withdrawal from the world

The slightest contacts [with the world] can do us harm, and unless we are very careful, and pay attention to what we say, what we do, and what we think, there will be an infinite number of reasons to overwhelm us with reproaches.

It is the deliberate withdrawal of the mind and intellect from outward, earthly, temporal things in order to focus them on the *eternalia* and the inward presence of God in the soul. On the other hand, this *Pensée* says nothing whatever about recollection, and the reason for that is that the editor has completely changed the subtitle that appears in M, though the text of the *Pensée* remains identical. In M the subtitle is "On the dangers of good works"—i.e. "On the dangers of what appear to us to be good works"—which is absolutely accurate.

[35] On Providence, see n. 6 above.

XXXII (32)

On the corruption of human beings[36]

When God leaves men and women to themselves, there are no limits to what they might do.

XXXIII (33)

That true confidence lies only in God

In this world there is no constancy nor any stability save that which is found in God, and in the confidence we have in his mercy and protection.

XXXIV (34)

On how we should regard humiliations[37]

We must bear in mind that it is God who humbles[38] us, and in this way we see that human beings are no more than instruments he wishes to use.

---

[36] As a Western Latin Christian, Rancé naturally accepted the Augustinian doctrine of the total depravity of human beings: we have inherited both the sin and the guilt of Adam, and the human race is no more than "one lump of sin" (see chap. 4, n. 2). Without grace, we cannot do a single good action, and, as Augustine said, "of our own power we can only fall" (see chap. 4, n. 3).

[37] At la Trappe, humiliations were a deliberate technique for training a monk, but a technique that could easily be misunderstood. The matter was discussed in chap. 1 above. See further David N. Bell, *Understanding Rancé: The Spirituality of the Abbot of La Trappe in Context*, Cistercian Studies Series 205 (Kalamazoo, MI: Cistercian Publications, 2005), 361, s.v. "Humility and humiliations." Marsollier and the editor of the *Pensées* are not thinking of humiliations as a deliberate technique, but rather as those humbling events that we inevitably experience in our lives and that, like the disgraces of *Pensées* 14, 62, 98, and 154, are ultimately good for us (though we certainly won't like them). The vital importance of humility has been discussed in chap. 1.

[38] The French verb *humilier* may mean to humiliate or to humble. In this *Pensée* (and given modern English usage) it is better to think of God humbling us rather than humiliating us. The discussion of humiliations continues in the next *Pensée*.

XXXV (35)

On the benefits of humiliations for those who are great in the world

Humiliations are useful for everyone, but essential for those who are great in the world, lest they puff themselves up and pay no heed to anything around them. This leads to pride, unless we keep careful watch on ourselves and do our utmost on all such occasions to take it upon ourselves to give to God what we know he asks, namely, that we strive to conquer ourselves. We may then have reason to hope that he, in his goodness, will look favorably on the efforts we make[39] to please him.

XXXVI (36)

On making good use of time

Since there is nothing more precious than time, there is nothing more important than using it as wisely as possible.

XXXVII (37)

On the wrong sort of zeal

Even in the holiest souls, the zeal for justice and truth degenerates into a zeal for acrimony, disquiet, and bitterness. The former gives life; the latter gives death.

XXXVIII (38)

On humility

We must recognize that everything we have comes from God, and thank him for it. The most unworthy thing of all is to claim for ourselves what is purely from him and what[40] does not belong to us.

---

[39] M: *les efforts que l'on fait*; P: *les efforts qu'on se fait.*
[40] M: *ce qui*; P: *qui.*

XXXIX (39)

On following God's ways

For those souls whose care and concern is their salvation, there is nothing to which they should apply themselves more than knowing the ways that the mercy of God opens for them, and following [those ways] without paying the slightest heed to anything that might impede them.

XL (40)

On making good use of graces

The greatest of all misfortunes is not making holy use of the graces that God offers us.

XLI (41)

That tears are necessary in repentance [41]

Sins for which we have never wept continue to exist in the eyes of God: only tears can wash them away. [42] It is by penitence [43] and changing our way of life [44] that we apply to ourselves the merits of the blood of Jesus Christ, and the self-indulgent way in which we habitually treat ourselves serves only to bring upon us a more severe judgment.

XLII (42)

On hating sin and doing good works

It is a very good thing to hate sin, but we must join to this hatred those virtues that are the opposite of our past errors; for virtue consists not only in fleeing evil, but in doing good.

---

[41] In French, *pénitence* can mean inward penitence or repentance or outward penance. *Faire pénitence*, for example, is "to do penance." The translation therefore depends on the context, and sometimes all three meanings may be included. See Bell, *Saint in the Sun*, 544.

[42] See chap. 5, n. 35.

[43] *La penitence*: see n. 41 above.

[44] *La conversion*: see n. 8 above.

XLIII (43)

That worldly honors can be useful

Worldly honors do not dispense us from the maxims and laws of the Gospel. They are often the means that God puts in our hands so that we might carry out [what the Gospel demands] more faithfully.

XLIV (44)

On holy indifference [45]

The way to die to ourselves and our self-love is to strip ourselves voluntarily of every attachment we can have for earthly things.

XLV (45)

On the benefits of humiliations [46]

At the Judgment of God, the only thing that will distinguish one person from another will be their[47] virtues, or, more accurately, all those virtues that the world wants to know least, namely, the love of humiliations and ignominy.

XLVI (46)

On loving our neighbor

We should take the greatest care in all our dealings with our neighbors lest we displease God and force him to close his hand because we have not shown to others that justice, charity, and compassion so highly commended.

XLVII (47)

On correcting our faults

It is a good thing to know our faults, but the greatest fault is not to do all that we can to correct them.

---

[45] What Rancé means by *indifférence* is examined in chap. 6.

[46] See n. 37 above.

[47] *Les vertus* "the virtues" in P is undoubtedly an error for M's *leurs vertus* "their virtues."

XLVIII (48)

On belonging wholly to God

We must belong to God in time in order to belong to him in eternity.

XLIX (49)

That temptations can be useful

If God allows us to be subjected to temptations, this is not that they might bring us down, but that by overcoming them we might become better and more worthy to receive new graces.

L (50)

On profiting from human injustice

It is sometimes useful to find ourselves treated unjustly by people from whom we should expect only evidences of charity. It shows us how little stock we can put in human beings.

LI (51)

That we need violence to carry off heaven [48]

The way to heaven is filled with difficulties, and the only way to smooth them out is by resisting our natural inclinations.

---

[48] The basis for this *Pensée* is Matt 11:12: *A diebus autem Joannis Baptistæ usque nunc, regnum cælorum vim patitur, et violenti rapiunt illud,* "From the days of John the Baptist until now, the kingdom of heaven suffers violence, and the violent carry it off." The French *ravir* in the subtitle directly parallels the Latin *rapiunt.* What the author is saying is that the way to heaven demands a violent and continual attack on our natural desires and inclinations. See also *Pensée* 78.

LII (52)

That prayers should be joined with good works[49]

Prayers are of little use if they are not accompanied by the faithful performance of our works.

LIII (53)

On submission to God's will

When we will only what God wills, then whatever may happen, we are always content, and unless we are prepared to offer up[50] our own works to him, we never serve him.

LIV (54)

That peace is to be found only in God

Peace consists uniquely in the submission of our hearts to the commands of him who is their sovereign master.

LV (55)

On trust in God

We often ruin the things we do by taking so little care to await their consequences from the hand of God. There is hardly any point in talking to people if we do not talk to God.

---

[49] There are three different subtitles for this *Pensée*. M¹ has "Prayers and good works [are] useful (*utiles*)"; M² has "Prayers and good works joined together (*unies*)"; P simply has "Prayers and good works." Of the three, that in M² is clearly the most appropriate.

[50] Lit. "make a sacrifice of (*faire un sacrifice*)."

LVI (56)

On the usefulness of good works

God is not satisfied simply with our will, but with our works: works that are full and according to his measure.[51]

LVII (57)

On loving truth

Truths are like streams of water: to have them in their purity we must follow them back to their fountainhead.[52]

LVIII (58)

On contempt for the world

Anyone who thinks on God and has some hope of eternity should never cast a single approving glance on even the greatest and most beautiful things the world has to offer.

LIX (59)

On desiring nothing but God

Those who in this world desire anything other than God, whatever their excuse may be, will live their lives in disquiet and end them in confusion.

LX (60)

On the dangers of the world

Those who seek tranquility of heart by relying on external things will never find true [tranquility]. They think up all manner of things that may best satisfy them, but not one of these will give them what their imagination portrays.

---

[51] See Luke 6:38: "Give, and it will be given to you: a good measure, pressed down, shaken together, and running over will be given into your lap. For with the measure you use, it will be measured back to you."

[52] The version in M is slightly longer: "we must always (*toujours*) follow them back to their source and fountainhead."

LXI (61)

On complete[53] *submission to God*

The only way of achieving happiness both inside and outside the monastery[54] is to accept everything that happens to us with equal submissiveness, to take care that we have no preference in our inclinations for one thing or another, and to respect in everything the orders of divine Providence.[55] [Providence] is usually treating us more mercifully when it allows things to happen to us that are[56] the very least of what our heart desires.

LXII (62)

On the benefits of disgrace and sickness

Sickness and disgrace are sure signs that God never tires of being merciful to us. He visits all those whom he afflicts, and the best thing he can do for us in this world, especially when we have had the misfortune to offend him, is to allow us to satisfy his justice and make amends for our past flaws by leading us by paths that are hard, rough, and contrary to our own inclinations.

LXIII (63)

On the usefulness of penances that God himself imposes on us[57]

Since God is the cause of the reconciliation of sinners, it is for him to impose on them the conditions [for their reconciliation] and to open up the way for them. If we follow our own reasoning in this, we will never fail to be led astray, however well intended we may have been in searching for them.

---

[53] P omits "complete (*entière*)."

[54] "both inside and outside the monastery." The French has *dans l'un & dans l'autre monde*, "in the one and in the other world," but it cannot possibly mean this world and the next. What follows wholly precludes that.

[55] See n. 6 above.

[56] M² changes the present *sont* "are" to the future *seront*, "will be."

[57] I.e. as distinct from penances we choose for ourselves, or (in the monastery) that are chosen for us by a superior. We may compare *Pensée* 15.

LXIV (64)

On submission to the will of God

The reasoning of sinners lacks light: they do not know what they do. Their blindness is the result of their sin, and the only way they can be safe is to let themselves be led to the ways[58] of Providence, to apply themselves to knowing it, and to respect and follow its movements.

LXV (65)

On the benefits of afflictions

Afflictions are the clearest indications we could possibly have of the care God takes in sanctifying us. Nature tells us that they serve no purpose. Faith teaches us that they are necessary. It follows, then, that there is nothing we ought to desire more, since we are required to live according to the light of faith, not according to our natural inclinations.

LXVI (66)

That we should not put much stock in worldly things

Human things appear charming and wonderful when viewed from afar, but when we see and savor them close up they are anything but what we hoped they would be. It is a consequence of God's mercy that he so arranges the things that pass away that there is not one of them that is not mixed with some bitterness.

LXVII (67)

On unexpected deaths

It is a great misfortune when the unexpected deaths of worldly people fail to make an impression on us, and do not impel us

---

[58] M: *au cours*; P: *au goût*. *Goût* "taste" is certainly an odd substitution for *cours*.

to work with greater care and diligence towards our own salvation.[59]

LXVIII (68)

On being too concerned with earthly goods[60]

It is in the order of God that someone in charge of a family
should take whatever care is necessary in managing and maintaining temporal things, but it is never permitted to carry these
same cares to the extent that they cause anxiety and agitation.
Such anxiety is a sure sign that they have found in our hearts
a place they should never occupy. To see the things of this
world in their true light, we must think of them as we will
see them at the very moment [of death], when they will be of
no further use to us—that is to say, without being affected by
them and totally ready to suffer their loss without regret or
complaint.

LXIX (69)

On the dangers of high society[61]

Just as it is impossible to stay perfectly well in places where
the corruption of the air brings about sickness,[62] there are also

---

[59] M continues here with a sentence entirely omitted in P: "From all eternity,
one man must die for the good of the people [see John 11:50; 18:14], but we
can say that every day God sacrifices a great number for the sanctification of
his Elect." In my own view the omission is justified: the *Pensée* is better without it.

[60] M adds "which is dangerous."

[61] "High society": *le grand monde* in both M and P.

[62] The idea that bad air could bring about sickness dates back to Galen and
Hippocrates. It was standard thinking throughout the Middle Ages and was
still current long after Rancé and Marsollier were dust. "It cannot be denied,"
wrote a learned contributor to *The Scots Magazine* in October 1796, "that the
effluvia of marshes is highly deleterious [*sic*], nor, that the vapours arising
from the filth of streets, are equally noxious, as being of a similar nature"
(*The Scots Magazine* 58 [1796]: 662).

certain aberrations of the heart that we cannot avoid in high society, and that remain despite every effort we can make to remedy them. The world is a field in which they find such an abundance of nourishment that we only ever attack them too weakly. And what is even more troublesome is that, in general, their development is as imperceptible as their birth, and we only discover them when they have already wreaked havoc within us and done us real harm.

LXX (70)

That God is our center, and that we must reunite with him [63]

Things are at rest when they are in their place and the situation natural to them. Our heart's [natural place] is God's heart, and when we are in his hand with our will in submission to his, our anxieties must necessarily cease and our restlessness come to an end. We shall then find ourselves wholly at peace and in perfect tranquility. [64]

LXXI (71) [65]

On patience

We must suffer in peace what we cannot avoid. God tolerates wicked people so that those who are good may always have something on which to exercise their charity. [66] Their wickedness should cause us grief, but not anger. We must hate the error, not the one who commits it. [67]

[63] M has *en lui*; P has *à lui*.

[64] In the text it is our anxieties and restlessness that find themselves in peace and tranquility, but since they are *our* anxieties and restlessness I felt entitled to amend the subject of the last sentence to "we."

[65] M (both editions) omits the number, certainly by accident, but the subtitle and text are identical in both M and P.

[66] The nature of charity (*charité*), as distinct from love (*amour*), is discussed in chap. 6.

[67] We may compare Augustine, *Epistola* 211.11; PL 33:962: *Cum dilectione hominum et odio vitiorum*, "With love for humankind and hatred of sins."

LXXII (72)[68]

On loving the world

There is nothing pleasant about the world and nothing to warrant our lingering there. God takes the greatest care to disfigure it so as to prevent us from loving it and becoming attached to it. Nevertheless, this deformity fails to disgust people, and from the way in which they live in the world, it seems that there is nothing there that does not captivate their hearts. They conform to it, they approve of its principles and sentiments, and there are very few who are not eager to give themselves up to its affairs and pleasures.

LXXIII (73)[69]

On the benefits of tribulations

If we live our lives without any conflict or opposition,[70] we will be subject to the greatest of all temptations, namely, that we have nothing to suffer from the hands of human beings. For it is written that those who belong to God and make their profession to serve him must pass through trials to purify their hearts,[71] and that this is the only way by which they can make themselves worthy of the good things and benefits that he intends for them both in time and in eternity.

"Hate the sin and not the sinner" was not said by Jesus Christ but by Mahatma Gandhi.

[68] M: LXXI.

[69] M: LXXII.

[70] "without any conflict or opposition" renders the French *sans contradiction*.

[71] See 1 Pet 1:6-7.

LXXIV (74)[72]

That God speaks to us through death[73]

Those who die either a good or a bad death often die more for [the benefit of] those they leave behind in the world than for themselves.

LXXV (75)[74]

On the need for good works

We must ask God for strength as well as instruction. It is certainly of great benefit when he enlightens us, but[75] that is not enough. We must also constrain him by our prayers to have us enter the path he has opened up for us, for those who find grace in his eyes will not be those who merely listen to his words, but those who put them into practice.

LXXVI (76)[76]

On contempt for the world

We must rejoice when we are at odds with our fellow men. It is a very valuable means [of spiritual training], provided we use it to be on good terms with God.

[72] M: LXXIII.

[73] The background to this brief *Pensée* is the idea, so important in seventeenth- and eighteenth-century France, of the "good death." We discussed the matter in chap. 4. The public spectacle of a "good death," with all its accoutrements, could be an edifying experience for a large number of people.

[74] M: LXXIII.

[75] P omits *but*.

[76] M², but not M¹, accidentally omits the number of this *Pensée*, though the subtitle and text are identical in both M and P. After this *Pensée*, we now have three different sets of numbering.

LXXVII (77)[77]

On the benefits of conflict and opposition[78]

The more we are raised up in this world, the more we need conflict and opposition. Only that can repress the malevolent states of mind that are the consequences of greatness.

LXXVIII (78)

That God gives a hundredfold[79]

Even in this world[80] God will repay a hundredfold the violence we do to ourselves to please him.[81]

LXXIX (79)

On God alone[82]

It is only God who deserves the attention of those who make their profession to belong to him and serve him.[83]

---

[77] From here to *Pensée* 165, the enumeration in M[1] is one less than in P, and in M[2] two less than in P.

[78] See n. 70 above: "conflict and opposition" = *contradictions*.

[79] The background to this *Pensée* is Mark 10:29-30: "Jesus answering, said: 'Truly I say to you, there is no one who has left house, or brothers, or sisters, or father, or mother, or children, or lands, for my sake and for the Gospel, who shall not receive a hundred times as much, now in this time (*nunc in tempore hoc*): houses, and brothers, and sisters, and mothers, and children, and lands, with persecutions; and in the world to come everlasting life.'" In other words, for those who have given up all for Christ and the Gospel, there are great rewards both in this world and the next.

[80] *Dès ce monde même* echoes the Vulgate *nunc in tempore hoc*.

[81] The violence we do to ourselves has already been explained in *Pensée* 51.

[82] The subtitle in both M and P is simply *Dieu seul*: see n. 31 above.

[83] *Faire profession* would normally refer to the formal act of profession made by a monk or a nun. In the *Pensées*, however, it may refer to the dedicated intention of any man or woman to follow in the footsteps of Christ, whether inside or outside the monastery. See also *Pensées* 73 and 86.

LXXX (80)

That trustworthy consolation[84] *[is to be found only]*
in imitating Jesus Christ[85]

The only trustworthy[86] consolation in this world lies in listening to Jesus Christ and imitating him. All other [consolations] are no more than delusions.

LXXXI (81)

On faithfulness

There is nothing more pleasing to God than souls who love to perform their duties[87] and who neglect nothing in the things to which they have willingly subjected themselves.

LXXXII (82)

On delaying our conversion[88]

We must not wait until the very last moment to put our most important affairs in order. In that state it is very difficult to put in order what is demanded of us by our conscience and the knowledge that we are about to appear before the Judgment of God.

---

[84] In Rancé's time, *consolation* could simply mean comfort or solace, but, especially in the plural, it was a technical term of seventeenth-century French spirituality. Consolations are "God's warm, peaceful, joyful, encouraging visitations which effect tears of love, repentant sorrow, a desire for heavenly things, prompter service of God, and affectively intensify faith, hope and love" (*A Dictionary of Christian Spirituality*, ed. Gordon S. Wakefield [London: SCM Press, 1983], 94). Some consolations are transitory, such as the tears that lead to a greater love of God. Some produce a permanent change of state, such as the continual experience of an indescribable inner joy that can never be lost even in the midst of adversity. See further Bell, *Saint in the Sun*, 540–41. In the *Pensées* I have always translated *consolation/s* by consolation/s.

[85] In M[1] the subtitle is simply "Consolation." In M[2] the subtitle has been omitted altogether.

[86] *Solide*: "strong, firm, stable, reliable, unswerving, trustworthy."

[87] P: "their duty" in the singular.

[88] I.e. On delaying changing our way of life: see n. 8 above.

LXXXIII (83)

On not paying heed to eternity

There are those who think only about the things that happen in the world and rarely turn their thoughts to eternity, despite the fact that this is the only thing that should occupy our spirit and our heart. Almost all people are walking on paths that mislead them, and everything they do is exactly the opposite of what they ought to do.

LXXXIV (84)

On keeping death in mind

At the moment of death, everything will be unimportant: the only thing that will remain is what we have done[89] in the eyes of God. This is something we should often say to ourselves, for even those who are most strongly convinced of it often think and act as if their convictions were quite the contrary.

LXXXV (85)

On detachment[90]

Those who truly belong to God find in him alone all that they need, and they have no difficulty in understanding what little justice[91] they receive from men and women.

LXXXVI (86)

On the same

Worldly goods are [always] accompanied by disagreeable circumstances, and they have everything they need to entangle those who either have them or seek them with a restlessness

---

[89] P changes the word order here, but there is no difference in meaning.

[90] *Détachement*: see n. 8. This, as we have said, is one of the principal themes of the *Pensées*.

[91] Or "fairness," "integrity," "being treated fairly or justly."

wholly inappropriate for those who make their profession[92] to serve God.

LXXXVII (87)

On the same

However great the benefits this world has to offer, we must give them up. They do not extend our days by a single moment, and those who die with something of faith and religion regret having attached themselves to them[93] when they must leave them forever. It is a grave deception to give the least space in our heart to something that hardly deserves to be there at all. The sole business of those who believe in eternity and desire it should be to prepare themselves for it by a heartfelt detachment from everything that passes away.

LXXXVIII (88)

On how people are misled

We often imagine that we are doing for God what we are actually doing for ourselves, and there is nothing more common than to have God serve as a pretext[94] for our own interests and satisfaction. In our blindness we think that we find truth and justice where there is none to be found.

LXXXIX (89)

On faithfulness

God loves souls who are faithful to him, who make their paths straight;[95] and the care that we take to respond to his graces draws down upon us further [graces].[96] The more we give back

---

[92] See n. 83 above.

[93] *De ne s'y être attachés* in M[1] has been corrected to *de s'y être attachés* in M[2] and P.

[94] M: *couverture*; P: *prétexte*. *Couverture* can mean a cloak or pretext, but *prétexte* is clearer.

[95] See Prov 3:6; Heb 12:13.

[96] M: *en attire l'augmentation*; P: *en attirent d'autres*. The meaning is the same.

to him, the more he gives, and we can say that he takes pleasure in filling to overflowing[97] those souls who show their gratitude to him.[98]

XC (90)

On forgiving our enemies

The feature that distinguishes those who belong to God from those who do not is pardoning and forgiving wrongs and affronts,[99] and what characterizes [true] Christians is that they have no memory, no recollection, and no resentment [of how they have been wronged]. To be convinced of this truth and to put it into practice is the clearest and surest indication we may have of our predestination.[100]

XCI (91)

On charity

It is ever the duty of charity to regard all human intentions in the best light possible, and it is better to be wrong in believing something to be good when it is not than in letting ourselves believe something to be evil when it may well be that there is[101] nothing evil there. The desire of charity is to avoid anything

---

[97] See Luke 6:38 cited in n. 51 above.

[98] *Les âmes reconnoissantes.* It is not enough simply to be passively grateful. God expects us to respond actively to his graces and show our gratitude to him by what we do in practice. He will then bestow on us further graces, and so on, and so on. This is a theme that occurs a number of times in the *Pensées*. Ingratitude to God, says Rancé, is "the most common and the most unpardonable sin" (*Pensée* 126).

[99] "wrongs and affronts" = *les injures*.

[100] I.e., that, by grace, one belongs to God's Elect and may look forward to eternal life in Paradise. Anyone who accepts the Augustinian principle of the total depravity of humankind (see n. 36 above) must inevitably accept the doctrine of predestination. That the doctrine gives rise to a host of theological problems is not in doubt, but Rancé does not discuss them. He would have regarded such discussion as dangerous and a total waste of time (see *Pensée* 207 and its accompanying note).

[101] M¹ and P both have *il n'y en a point* (present); M² has *il n'y en auroit point* (conditional).

that can cause unpleasantness, and that we say only what can contribute to the calming and appeasing of the [human] spirit.

XCII (92)
On the benefits of afflictions

God allows us to experience difficulties we should never expect in order to exercise our virtue and strengthen in us the state of mind in which we ought to exist. That is, that we need to preserve the peace to look upon God, and [understand] everything we encounter on our path as coming to us by the disposition of Providence,[102] to which we are duty bound to submit.

XCIII (93)
That greatness can be useful

If God has made us great in this world, it is only that we may use our position to make ourselves great in heaven. This must be our goal in all that we do, and all our activities in this life must be directed to this good alone.

XCIV (94)
On flight from the world

Not everyone is obliged to follow the advice to leave the world [for a monastery], but the fact that we should have no love for the world is an indispensable obligation for every man and woman. It is also an obligation as binding upon those who occupy the highest ranks among us as on those who occupy the least.

---

[102] See n. 6 above.

XCV (95)

On trusting in God

All we need do is to put ourselves entirely in God's hands,[103] and when that is done, we have the right to hope for everything from his mercy. He foresees our needs and anticipates all our necessities.

XCVI (96)

On advancing in perfection

A Christian's life should be one of continual progress, for God wants those who have the happiness to belong to him to do their utmost to belong to him even more. It is in this way that they show him how much they value his gifts and the marks of his mercy.

XCVII (97)

On trusting in God

Happy are those who cling to Jesus Christ alone, who accept all that they receive in submission and holy indifference,[104] and [who regard] everything that happens to them as coming from his hand. This is the way to live in unchanging tranquility, and successfully to avoid all the problems that are the inevitable consequences of the different things that happen to us. A

---

[103] Lit. "one need only abandon oneself (*s'abandonner*) to God." The term *abandon*, writes J. Neville Ward (and his brief account cannot be bettered), was used by certain seventeenth-century French writers "for the trusting acceptance of God's providence and the cooperation with him in obedience which together were seen as essential Christianity" (*Dictionary of Christian Spirituality*, 1). "It is that giving of oneself to God," Ward continues, "in which one wishes to do his will whatever the situation and at the same time not only accepts the situation as the current context for this but actively wills it, as it were endorses it, since faith interprets it not as mere happening but as divine providence" (2).

[104] See n. 45 above.

Christian ought to have the solidity of a pillar built on rock[105]—
that is to say, on trust in Jesus Christ—and not the pliability of
a reed that bends and changes at the mercy of the wind.

XCVIII (98)

On useful disgraces

Disgrace and privations are the sure means given us by God
to gain eternity. Those who regard them in this way never
know unhappiness, and what they await takes the place of
everything that can be taken away from them by the envy and
injustice of men and women.

XCIX (99)

On [finding] peace in God

When we have no desires, then whatever may happen, we are
always at peace, because we will only what God wills, and
that his will be always done. It is God to whom we must look[106]
in all things, and to whom we must subject ourselves.

C (100)

On the nothingness[107] of worldly things

The span of everything here below is so short and uncertain
that there is nothing that can bring about real joy or real sorrow,
save that which takes away from or that which adds to the
glory of Jesus Christ. If he were before our eyes as much as he
should be, and if his views ruled our sentiments and our conduct, the only consolations[108] we would experience in this
world would come from conforming to his will and accepting
with complete abandonment[109] everything that Providence

[105] See Matt 7:24-25; Luke 6:48.
[106] M: *on doit regarder*; P: *il faut regarder*, which is stronger: "one must" as
against "one should."
[107] Or "emptiness" (*néant*).
[108] See n. 84 above.
[109] *Dans un abandonnement entier*: see n. 103 above.

disposes. [In this way] whatever people treat as strokes of misfortune will be for us strokes of blessings and graces.

CI (101)

That we must prove by our works that the world is nothing

To be convinced of the vanity of the world[110] is not enough: we must act in accordance with our belief. It is a great misfortune to live as if we esteemed what we know should not be esteemed. To act in this way would clearly be contrary to the dictates of our conscience.

CII (102)

That virtue stands firm against every trial

Virtue is like a great tree that puts down the deepest roots and, when it is battered by the force of the winds, grows ever stronger.

CIII (103)

On the advantage of solitude

Happy are they whom God has withdrawn from the world, and who await in the solitude [of the monastery], as under his protecting wings,[111] the end of these days of misfortune and iniquity.

CIV (104)

That keeping our eyes on eternity
should console us for the evils of this life

If we have in our mind's eye that incorruptibility promised us by God, that should provide us with consolation from all the evil things that might happen to us, and destroy in our hearts any desire[112] for things that are not eternal.

---

[110] See Eccl 1:2.
[111] See Ps 56:2; 90:4.
[112] M¹ alone has the plural: *tous désirs*.

CV (105)

On useful sufferings

There is but one code of conduct to adopt, and that is to love[113] God's orders and to accept them not only with patience, but with the joy that the testimony of our conscience should produce in us when we suffer for the love of him, and do whatever we do to please him.

CVI (106)

On peace[114]

The way to preserve peace is to be perfectly detached from everything outside of ourselves, and to permit within ourselves only what has been put there by God.

CVII (107)

On the duty of monks[115] *[and nuns] to be totally detached*[116]

Anything [other than Christ] that occupies a heart that is bound[117] to Jesus Christ by an obligation as eternal and holy as that of [monastic] vows always casts it into agitation and confusion, for such things take up space to which they have no right and, as a result, they draw [the heart] away from the order established by God. It is a disruption that, however insignificant it may appear, has unfortunate results, and it never fails to cause anxiety and unrest in all those in whom it is to be found. Those who are consecrated to God by their [monastic] state, but who seek relief and consolations from external things against the enemies and temptations to be found in cloisters,

---

[113] The verb is *adorer* "to adore, worship."

[114] M²: "On peace in perfect detachment (*dégagement*)."

[115] *Des religieux*: the noun is masculine plural, but in French that may include male and female religious. This is one of the very few *Pensées* addressed specifically to professed monks and nuns.

[116] *Sur le dégagement entier.*

[117] M: *engagé*; P: *attaché.*

have less repose and tranquility than the others. Indeed, the more they devote themselves to what they think can alleviate their difficulties, the more they increase and multiply them, and, putting it bluntly, they impoverish themselves instead of enriching themselves. [And why?] Because God is their treasure, and it is he alone whom they should have in mind. All else is no more than an abyss of evils and misery.

CVIII (108)

On the nothingness[118] *of the world*

Having any converse with the world is a waste of time: there is nothing[119] to be gained. [The world] is so powerless that it is utterly unable to give us anything that can offer us any satisfaction.

CIX (109)

On being faithful to God

God will give himself to us in direct proportion to the faithfulness and care that we take in turning our face from the world. In drawing away from the world, we come closer to God, and in confirming our divorce from the former, we confirm our marriage to the latter.

CX (110)

On being indifferent to the way people judge us

The approval or disapproval of men and women should not be of the least concern to those whose minds are occupied with the judgments of Jesus Christ.

---

[118] Or "emptiness": see n. 107 above.

[119] *On y gagne rien* in M¹ is amended to *on n'y gagne rien* in M² and P.

CXI (111)

On the benefits of sufferings

The joy of the disciples of Jesus Christ is to be like their master, to follow him in his sufferings, and to be, as was he, the object of the hatred, inhumanity, and rage of those who were the enemies of his glory and his name.

CXII (112)

That faith protects us against the evils of this life

The evils that we suffer, together with those that threaten us, should serve only to increase our faith and our courage, and the trust we should have in the promises of Jesus Christ should provide us with true consolation.

CXIII (113)

That a well-regulated and hard life is useful for salvation

A well-ordered life[120] has special merit before God, for it may truly be said that when we subject ourselves [to him] in this way, we win an unending victory over ourselves, for all our natural inclinations lead us to seek relief in change and variation.

CXIV (114)

On the benefits of prayer

Prayer is no less necessary for preserving the life of the soul than breathing is for preserving the life of the body. Christians continue and make progress in the ways of God only in proportion to how much they pray.

---

[120] In the subtitle the expression is *une vie égale*, "a balanced, regular life"; here it is *une vie réglée*, "a steady, regulated life." In both cases, it is life lived according to a rule—not necessarily a monastic rule, but a rule one might make for oneself in consultation with a spiritual director.

CXV (115)

That to pray well we must be detached from the world

God never fails to give the grace and spirit of prayer to those who present themselves before his eyes truly detached and disassociated[121] from anything that may displease him. Nothing is more effective than this emptiness and poverty[122] in drawing to us the abundance of his riches. To pray well we must have poverty in our life and faithfulness in our conduct.

CXVI (116)

On the folly of the world [123]

The world speaks and passes off its fantasies as truths. It takes as little[124] to know it as to give it any[125] credence.

CXVII (117)

On the unreliability of the human spirit and heart

There is nothing certain about anything that happens here below, and the human heart is in itself wholly capricious and fickle. It follows that we should never stop asking God to preserve and strengthen us on the path he has had us enter.

---

[121] *Dans un dégagement & dans une désoccupation véritable.*

[122] Both here and in the next sentence, poverty (*pauvreté*) is poverty of spirit rather than an absence of material goods. Being empty and poor in spirit means that we have no more self-will or self-love, and are therefore wholly detached or disassociated from the things of this world. Monks and nuns, of course, were poor in a material sense, since they were forbidden personal possessions, but unless it is freely and deliberately chosen, material poverty can easily lead to an overwhelming desire to possess what one does not have. In other words, it can lead to a greater attachment to, rather than any detachment from, the things of this world. But as the subtitle says, *Pour bien prier il faut être détaché du monde*, "To pray well one must be detached from the world."

[123] See 1 Cor 3:19.

[124] *Pour* in M[1] is corrected to *peu* in M[2] and P.

[125] M[1] omits *de* in *de croyance.*

CXVIII (118)

On the danger of involvement with the world

To the extent that the world gives us no pleasure, it is not to be feared. But when we begin to grow too familiar with it, and when there is nothing left in it that seems alien to us, then it is dangerous and we must be on our guard.

CXIX (119)

That keeping eternity in our sights can destroy
the misleading ideas produced by the world

Since we ought to live and reign with Jesus Christ in eternity, it is only right that we should live only for him in time, and flee from people, the sight of whom alone can ruin the best and most holy resolutions. The world is nothing but malice: it spreads it abroad everywhere, and, for the little time that we are here, it is very difficult to ward off its pernicious impact.

CXX (120)

On judging ourselves severely

There is nothing that induces God more to judge us with mercy than to judge ourselves with severity. And if our sense of justice does not always lead us to accuse ourselves [in this way], it is at least a clear indication of our will to be just.

CXXI (121)

That there is little to worry about in the way people judge us

When we are sure that there is nothing blameworthy in what people are pleased to reprove and condemn, the only course to take[126] is to remain at peace [in ourselves]. We would be very weak or very unfortunate if we allowed our peace of mind to

---

[126] M: *suivre* "to follow"; P: *prendre* "to take."

depend on the fancies of those who think they have some sort of right to judge what we do[127] unfairly and in an unenlightened way.

CXXII (122)

That the world follows us everywhere to persecute us

It is not enough to erase the world from our memory so as to be no longer in its [memory], and all the trouble we take to forget it produces little more than the fact that most of our friends easily forget us. But as for those who do not do[128] this, they always remember [the world].

CXXIII (123)

On the danger of praise

If we always bear in mind that the only real glory is that of God, we will be more miserly and more circumspect when it comes to ascribing it to people, who are usually condemned by God for the very things by which they draw to themselves the approval of the world.

CXXIV (124)

On the same

Praise is much more dangerous than defamation. It takes much less courage to feel the ill effects of an insult than the malign influence of a compliment.

[127] Lit. "to judge present things (*choses présentes*)."
[128] *Sont* in P is a typographical error for *font*, as in M. I.e. those who do not try to forget the world.

CXXV (125)

On the weight of graces[129]

The weight of graces has a heaviness we cannot comprehend. We cannot say how many people will be condemned by what should actually lead to their sanctification.[130]

CXXVI (126)

On ingratitude towards God [131]

The most common and the most unpardonable sin of men and women is ingratitude, for to put it plainly, there is not a moment in our life when God does not open upon us the hands of his mercy, and there is not a moment when we have not given him evidence of our obduracy. The world is the kingdom of ingrates, and God does nothing but rain and sow on sinners.[132]

---

[129] The typesetter of M[2] has gone astray here. In M[1] and P "On ingratitude towards God" correctly follows "On the weight of graces." In M[2] the subtitle "On ingratitude towards God" takes the place of "On the weight of graces," and the subtitle for what should be "On ingratitude towards God" is omitted altogether.

[130] We may compare *ps.*-Anselm of Canterbury, *De mensuratione crucis*, v; PL 159:297D: *Pondus gratiae humiliat et deprimit, cum consideramus quod ea indigni sumus, qui magis in inferno esse merueramus*, "The weight of grace humbles and overwhelms us when we consider that we are unworthy of it and that we deserve rather to be in hell." The term "weight of graces" (in the plural) appears nowhere in the Migne Patrology.

[131] M[2] omits the subtitle, which appears in error in *Pensée* 125.

[132] This is what the text says (*Dieu ne fait autre chose que de pleuvoir & de semer sur des pécheurs*), but what God is raining and sowing is not stated. Does he rain down his mercy on sinners, despite their ingratitude (see Matt 5:45), or does he rain down his wrath on sinners because of their ingratitude? The context seems to imply the former, but I am not at all sure what Rancé is saying here.

CXXVII (127)

On wishing others only the good things of eternity

We ought to wish our friends only the good things of eternity; for just as we cannot possess those of the world without danger, neither can we desire them for anyone else without scruple and fear.

CXXVIII (128)

That everything good comes from God

Whatever good we do is the work of God. It is not the result of our own virtue, but of his goodness alone. He makes of us whatever he pleases, without being hindered by our frailty or weakness.

CXXIX (129)

On the dangers of the world

The world is full of temptations and tempters, and it often happens that it is those who call themselves our best friends who set before us the most dangerous and unavoidable snares. All we need do to invite conflict is to wish for the good, and when people do not have good reasons for opposing it, they will summon up a multitude of bad ones to help them! It is not by argument that we withstand [these attacks], but by faithfulness and steadfastness of heart.

CXXX (130)

On the monastic way of life[133]

The monastic life[134] is a state so opposed to that of the world, and the paths followed there so contrary to the way followed

---

[133] *La vie religieuse*, "the religious life." In seventeenth-century France *religion* was a word of wide meaning. It could mean religion in general, the Christian religion in particular, religious belief, religious sentiment, religious faith, or (as here) the religious way of life, i.e. monasticism. The expression *entrer en religion* meant "to become a religious," i.e. a monk or nun.

[134] *La Religion*: see n. 133 above.

in the world, that we should not be surprised if one demands from those who have entered the cloister attitudes quite unknown to them. We might also wish [to see] in them now just as much obedience and submission as the attachment they once had to acting in accordance with their own self-will and abandoning themselves in everything to their own judgment.

CXXXI (131)

On the benefits of withdrawal [from the world]

Every day truths lose their strength in the human heart. Happy are those who are no longer of the world, but happier still those who never hear of it and know nothing of what happens there. It is enough to know that there is some person out there who deserves our compassion, and that we have an endless obligation to pray for that person without having a detailed knowledge of his or her wickedness and faults.

CXXXII (132)

That the spirit of the world is opposed to that of Jesus Christ

It is written that the world has no taste for the things of God and that the spirit of Jesus Christ and that [of the world] have nothing in common.[135] The latter approves what the former condemns; the latter scorns and rejects what the former seeks.[136] Happy are those who, by a blessed discernment, hear and cling to the voice that cannot deceive and who have no ears for what are no more than lies.

---

[135] See Rom 8:1-17; 1 Cor 2:12.
[136] M: *recherche*; P: *cherche*.

CXXXIII (133)

On trust in God

There is no difficulty we cannot overcome when we place ourselves unreservedly[137] in the hands of Jesus Christ and put all our trust and strength in him.

CXXXIV (134)

That for some people withdrawal [from the world] is dangerous

Withdrawal [from the world] is extremely useful if it is based on real needs. But there is no doubt at all that if it is undertaken without a sound basis and well-founded reasons, it may deprive us of yet greater help we might have in pleasing Jesus Christ and serving him faithfully.

CXXXV (135)

That the only true [peace] is peace of heart

Peace is the heart's treasure. It is by this that we possess God, for he cannot be found in restlessness and confusion. God's Elect will pass from peace in time to peace in eternity, for his Elect are those who love his law, and, according to his word,[138] it is they alone who may enjoy the most profound peace.

CXXXVI (136)

That a holy life prepares us for a holy death[139]

We must make ourselves worthy of a holy death by living a holy life, and[140] we must do what we believe can procure powerful protection for us from God in times of need. It is

---

[137] *quand on s'abandonne sans réserve*: see n. 103 above.

[138] Ps 118:165: *Pax multa diligentibus legem tuam*, "Much peace have those who love your law."

[139] The background to this *Pensée* is the idea of the "good death": see n. 73 above.

[140] M¹ omits "and."

useless to expect from God's goodness the grace to end well a life that we have lived wickedly.

CXXXVII (137)
On the benefits of sickness

The only reason that God visits us with the sicknesses he sends us is to have us appear before him when it pleases him to summon us. That is, when we do not respond to his intentions and the marks of his mercy that he bestows on us, and when he is not the sole object of our reflections and thoughts.

CXXXVIII (138)
On doing good

We will not render account to God for the good we have not done by the good we have not neglected to do.[141]

CXXXIX (139)
On the usefulness of afflictions

We ought to suffer whatever afflictions God sends us in time not only with resignation but with joy, since we have reason to believe that this is to spare us in eternity.

CXL (140)
On doing God's will[142]

Chief among all the good things of this world is doing the will of God.

---

[141] This *Pensée*, with its three negatives, is a little tricky. What it appears to say is that in the eyes of God the good that we actually do does not balance out the greater good that we should have done, but did not.

[142] This is the subtitle in P. M¹ has "The chief good (*le souverain bien*)"; M² omits the subtitle altogether.

CXLI (141)

On forgiving one's enemies

No one is ever without sin,[143] and if God puts up with us with our miseries, it is only just that we should bear with those of others.

CXLII (142)

On the benefits of afflictions

If people knew the real value of the afflictions of this life and how profitable they are [in preparing us] for death, they would be eager to seek them out.

CXLIII (143)

On the danger of neglecting our salvation

If people do not store up things for eternity, then whatever they may do is nothing but a destructive waste of time.

CXLIV (144)

That treating people as equals[144] is necessary and often useful

Treating people as equals is often useful and even necessary in very many encounters, for it is an effective means of averting and warding off great evils. There is yet more reason to use it when it tends only to raise a person to a stricter life and a more perfect piety.

---

[143] See 1 John 1:8.

[144] "treating people as equals" = *condescendance*/condescension. "Condescension" has something of a pejorative impact and is a misleading translation of *condescendance*. *Condescendance* is putting aside any power, position, or privileges one might have, and treating others as being on exactly the same level as oneself. In a society as rigidly stratified as seventeenth-century France, where everyone was highly conscious of his or her position, this was no small thing. The aristocracy, both civil and ecclesiastic, demanded and received a degree of deference unthinkable to most of us today, and for an archbishop (let us say) to treat a country *curé* as an equal was well nigh inconceivable.

CXLV (145)

That the truth is often concealed

Everyone wants to please, and hardly anyone wants to speak the truth.

CXLVI (146)

That we cannot please the world if we do not follow its maxims

We do not please those whom we do not wish to imitate, and those who walk in broad ways[145] cannot abide those who keep to ways that are more strict and more exacting.

CXLVII (147)

On keeping order in everything[146]

Those who live in confusion cannot avoid doing wrong.

CXLVIII (148)

That delaying our conversion[147] *is dangerous*

We are wrong to put off the matter of our salvation, and [wrong] to suppose that just a few moments are enough to prepare us for something that never ends, and that we appear before God but for an instant. No! It is forever, for eternity suffers neither change nor variation. There is no going back to make amends for past faults and transgressions. There remains only everlasting remorse and regret for having committed them, and then we repent uselessly for having preferred the vain amusements of the created order to the eternity of God, who alone should fill our hearts and be the unique object of our affections, our desires, and our thoughts.

---

[145] See Matt 7:13.
[146] The subtitle is omitted in M (both editions).
[147] I.e. changing our way of life: see n. 8 above.

CXLIX (149)

On having contempt for earthly things

It is a mistake and a terrible blindness to put the least value on things that appear but for a moment and then disappear, and to neglect those that never pass away. Eternity should be the sole concern of anyone who knows that there is such, and I cannot understand how anyone can pay the slightest heed to anything unconnected with it or that cannot lead us to it.

CL (150)

On the usefulness of afflictions

God has too much love for those who serve him and who belong to him to neglect their training. Nothing happens to them, either inwardly or outwardly, that does not provide them with some occasion to perform acts of submission, charity, acquiescence, or patience.

CLI (151)

On the benefits of serving God

In serving God and in perseverance[148] we find something that the whole world cannot give.[149]

---

[148] *La persévérance*. This is not just perseverance in a general sense, but the Augustinian doctrine of *donum perseverantiae*, the gift of perseverance, by which Augustine meant that those whom God has predestined to be saved are given not only the gift of true faith, but also the gift of persevering in faith "even to the end" (Matt 24:13) and not falling away. From a human point of view, says Augustine, it is impossible to know why, of two righteous people, one should be given the gift of final perseverance and the other not. But from a divine point of view, it must be the case that the one who perseveres is among the predestined while the other is not. Conversely, a failure to persevere indicates that one is not of God's Elect, but since one may fall away at any time, one cannot tell whether a person has persevered until they have died. For Augustine, then, a Christian cannot know with absolute certainty whether he or she is one of the Elect so long as they are still alive. This was not the view of John Calvin, but this is not the place for a comprehensive history of the doctrine of perseverance. All we need say here, with Rancé as with Augustine, is that perseverance is entirely a gift of God.

[149] M: *de nous donner*; P: *de donner*.

CLII (152)

On the injustice of judging falsely

The reason that we are so accustomed to cast blame on things that do not deserve blame is that we judge actions by what they appear to be and not by what they are in reality.

CLIII (153)

On the brevity of life

Since the good and bad things of this life both have an end, the latter are not worth fearing and the former are not worth desiring.

CLIV (154)

On being indifferent to the good and bad things of this life

The longest life lasts for but a moment, and it is a mistake to regard it as anything more than an insubstantial mist. Both reason and faith show us that there is no greater vanity or folly than to put value on a fleeting moment that is surrounded by time that knows neither measure nor limit. When we feel this in our heart, it eases all the afflictions that may happen to us. True Christians never grow weary of what the world calls disgrace and misfortune.[150]

CLV (155)

That we must advance in virtue

The life[151] of a Christian should be one of continual progress and improvement. The worst misfortune of all is to leave[152] God's work incomplete, for we can never return to finish it, and it stops there forever.

---

[150] M adds "&c."

[151] For *la vie* in P, M has *la vue*, which is possible. We might translate it as "The sights of a Christian should be fixed on continual progress. . . ." But *la vie* is better.

[152] Reading *laisser* with M. P has *saisir*, which does not make sense. It is almost certainly a typographical error.

CLVI (156)

On complete submission to God

Everything must yield to the orders of God, and our displeasure must be no less subject to his will than the lives of those whom we miss.[153] Nothing here below has any stability or duration, and we must always be ready to give back into his hands whatever he has put in ours.

CLVII (157)

On the terrible judgments of God

God's examination of all that we have done will be so wide-ranging and exacting that nothing [that we deem] righteous will stand before him. His mercy alone must determine what happens to us in eternity, and only he[154] can offer repose and consolation to those who are occupied with the thought of death. Trust opens the doors of the kingdom of Jesus Christ, and he will never close them[155] in the face of those who will appear there with no other worth[156] or merit than that of placing their hope in his goodness.

---

[153] This sentence was the most difficult of all the *Pensées* to translate. I consulted two native French speakers (both Cistercians of the Strict Observance) and an Associate Professor of French. The main problem is the meaning of *ressentiment*, which, in Rancé's time, could mean two quite contrary things: resentment (in the modern sense) and gratitude. In this *Pensée* both meanings are possible. The translation I have presented here represents the majority view, but I cannot guarantee that it is correct. Here is the French, the same in all editions: *Il faut que tout cède aux ordres de Dieu, & notre ressentiment ne doit pas être moins soumis à sa volonté, que l'a été la vie des personnes que nous regrettons.* In other words (and if the majority view is indeed correct), since everything is of limited duration, it follows that some whom we have known have died. We are naturally not too happy about this, but since their deaths could only have occurred in accordance with God's will, so our displeasure must also be subject to his will. In brief, as the subtitle has it, our ideal is complete submission to the will of God, whatever it may bring.

[154] In M it is only his mercy that can offer repose and consolation.

[155] M: *il ne les fermera point*; P: *il ne les fermera pas*. M is stronger.

[156] M: *ils n'auroient* (conditional) *d'autre dignité*; P: *ils n'auront* (future) *d'autre dignité*.

CLVIII (158)

On knowing the good and practicing it

If our enlightenment has borne no fruit, it will be our condemnation, and if we have known the truth but not followed it,[157] then God will judge us more harshly than if we had never known it at all.

CLIX (159)

On the dangers of the world

The holy rules by which we should lead our lives are unknown in the world, and those who are happy enough to be acquainted with them are not so [happy] as to overcome the obstacles they come up against in order to conquer their weakness and raise themselves above what they find established and legitimized by customs and habits that are almost universal.[158] To withdraw from the world is to seek refuge[159] from a tempest in which it is virtually impossible to avoid shipwreck.

CLX (160)

On the same

Ignorance of our obligations cannot be excused, and it does not shield us from the judgments of God.

CLXI (161)

On the dangers of the [Royal] Court

Those who frequent the Court[160] are unjust in their thinking, and [their thoughts] are always filled with malice. They are

---

[157] "But not followed it" has been accidentally omitted in P.

[158] In other words, knowing what one should do to overcome the dangers posed by the world does not mean that one will succeed in doing so. The sentence is rather cumbersome, but the whole of this *Pensée*—all twelve lines of it—is but one single sentence.

[159] M[1]: *se tirer*; M[2] and P: *se retirer*. They amount to the same thing.

[160] "Those who frequent the Court" = *les Courtisans*. A *courtisan* is a courtier; a *courtisane* is a courtesan. In seventeenth-century France, they were

like demons, playing each other false and being in agreement only when it comes to persecuting and oppressing those who are just.

CLXII (162)

That in one's youth one should beware of guiding others

In one's youth it is dangerous to take upon oneself the guidance of souls. It leads to people's building in vain, and what they raise up has neither stability nor duration. This is because they do not give themselves time to lay down those foundations without which one cannot build a solid structure.

CLXIII (163)

That faith reassures[161] us in times of spiritual aridity

God sometimes seems[162] to hide or suspend the protection we feel. We must then rely on our faith. It is our strength and the invisible arm on which we must support ourselves. It is useful to think about sickness when we are in good health, and, in a time of stillness and calm, to prepare ourselves to face a tempest!

CLXIV (164)[163]

On making our life useless

The worst possible use we can make[164] of life is to make ourselves equally unworthy of either living or dying.

---

sometimes the same thing and were referred to as *les grandes horizontales.*

[161] M[1]: *assure*; M[2] and P: *rassure*. The meaning here is the same.

[162] M: *semble*; P: *paroît*.

[163] M[2] has exactly the same subtitle as in M[1] and P, but accidentally omits the number.

[164] M: *nous faisons*; P: *l'on fait.*

CLXV (165)[165]
That God's help is essential

If God does not bless our works and take a hand in them, there is very little point in placing our hope in them.

CLXVI (166)
That we are filled with either God or the world

There can never be a void in our life. Everything in our heart that is not possessed by God must be taken over and usurped, as it were, by created things.

CLXVII (167)
That God penetrates our most inward being

God judges us by the most secret inclinations of our hearts; men and women know only the surface. But nothing can escape him who sees everything laid bare.

CLXVIII (168)
On human fickleness

The essential property of everything that happens in the world is to distract and divert us from the principal object we should always have before our eyes. We must appeal to God and ask him to stabilize our soul's volatility, and grant it that steadfastness that can only come from him. Of ourselves we are nothing but inconstancy and indecision, and we can say that since the Fall, created men and women[166] change without knowing why. Since they withdrew from God, who is the principle of all unchangeability, they have become as pliant as a reed.

---

[165] From here to the end, the enumeration in M¹ is one less than in P, and in M² three less than in P. The last *Pensée* is therefore numbered 258 in M¹, 256 in M², and 259 in P.

[166] "created men and women" = *la créature*.

CLXIX (169)

That the heart and the spirit are very different

It is the easiest thing to fill up the spirit[167] with great truths, while our hands remain as empty as if they had been stripped of every one of these illuminations.

CLXX (170)

On prayer

God wants us to ask him for what he has already determined to grant us, and it pleases him when we solicit his goodness.

CLXXI (171)

On human frailty

Human wisdom, however enlightened it may be, is of very little consequence if God does not bestow upon it his blessing. There is no true illumination save his, and without that all is but darkness, trouble, and confusion.

CLXXII (172)

That God reveals his glory in everything

Just as God created the world we see around us, in all its order, splendor, and beauty, out of dreadful chaos,[168] he knows just how to reveal his glory in things that seem to be the complete opposite. We must adore all that he does. We must preserve charity at all times, especially when we think we have reason to complain.

---

[167] Exactly what Rancé means by *esprit*/spirit depends on the context. Here it means the human mind. What he is saying here, as he says elsewhere in the *Pensées*, is that it is one thing to know "great truths"—what we should do—intellectually, but quite another to put them into practice. If we know them in our heart, however, which represents a far deeper, experiential level, then we may expect to see our hands respond and take appropriate action. Putting it in modern terms, knowing all the principles of brain surgery does not make one a brain surgeon.

[168] Gen 1:2.

CLXXIII (173)

That consolation[169] is to be found in God alone

Truly Christian souls and those who sincerely belong to Jesus Christ have no need of any human consolation for the tribulations that happen to them. When we have no desire but to follow what God has ordered, we find in him and in our submission to his will all that we need for our comfort. Our submissiveness is always superior to our sufferings, and the sacrifice we offer to God in the loss of those most dear to us is the quickest and most effective means we can employ not[170] only for our own consolation, but still more for the repose of those whose loss we regret.[171]

CLXXIV (174)

On preparing ourselves for death

Given that we often have so little time to prepare ourselves for death, it is never too soon to detach ourselves from this world so as to make ourselves deserving of eternity.

CLXXV (175)

That the good have little to fear from death

It is only those who have been[172] strictly vigilant and wholly faithful in their conduct who will not be troubled or surprised by the coming[173] of Jesus Christ.

---

[169] See n. 84 above.

[170] M¹ omits *not*.

[171] M: *elles regrettent*; P: *nous regrettons*.

[172] For the present *is* and perfect *have been* in P (*sont* and *ont gardé*), M has the future and future perfect (*seront* and *auront gardé*).

[173] Reading *la venue* with M for *la vue* "the sight, appearance" in P, though both are possible.

CLXXVI (176)
On attaching ourselves to eternal things
Instead of just producing in us a vain and totally useless feeling of sorrow, the uncertainty and changeability of all human affairs should be sufficient in itself to convince us that it is not to these things that we must attach ourselves, but only to those that are never subject to change.

CLXXVII (177)
That when it comes to worldly things, the inclinations of our spirit and of our heart are very different[174]
Although we may be convinced of the vanity of things here below and treat them with all the contempt they deserve, these trifles still impede us and occupy us as if they were of major consequence, and we spend our lives doing what we cannot stop condemning!

CLXXVIII (178)
On what needs to be done in our withdrawal [from the world]
Even though we have withdrawn [from the world], if we do not watch over ourselves with the greatest care and confine ourselves within the boundaries of our condition, it is to be feared that we will find, even in the depths of our solitude, those worldly trifles and empty nothings from which we thought we had separated ourselves for ever.

---

[174] In this *Pensée* the contrast between spirit and heart is exactly the same as in *Pensée* 169. What lodges in the spirit/mind is superficial, however true it may be, and it produces no results. What lodges in the heart sinks deep, is reflected in actions, and results in our spiritual advancement.

CLXXIX (179)

On the danger of making progress in our youth

There is always a risk in making progress before we have had time to acquire the necessary foundation and capacity, and nothing hinders us more from attaining the highest degree of virtue than to exhibit it[175] too soon.

CLXXX (180)

That keeping watch over ourselves is essential
in our withdrawal [from the world]

If we wish to find in the cloister the holy peace and repose that we seek, we must die to everything: not just to the world outside us, but even to that [world] we carry in the depths of our heart, in the secret places of our soul. Unless we do this we will meet in the solitude just the same evils and just the same feelings we wished to avoid when we separated ourselves from human society.

CLXXXI (181)

On obedience

The surest way [to spiritual advancement] and one in which we cannot be misled is to prefer in all things the will of our superiors to our own.[176]

CLXXXII (182)

On the love of God

God gives his hand to those who love him[177] and never withdraws it, and the love we have for him engages his good-

---

[175] M: *l'expose*; P: *s'expose*.

[176] This *Pensée* is neither more nor less than a single sentence summary of Chapter 5, *De oboedientia*, of the Rule of Saint Benedict.

[177] There is an important difference here between M and P. M has "those who love him" (*ceux qui l'aiment*) while P has "those whom he loves" (*ceux qu'il aime*). Given what follows in the *Pensée* about the effects of our love, it seems to me that M offers a better reading.

ness, links us with his justice, and does holy violence to his mercy.[178]

CLXXXIII (183)

On the dangers of conversations

There is nothing that dries up the heart more or is more destructive to piety[179] than useless conversations. Those who truly love conversing with God maintain a profound silence with human beings.

CLXXXIV (184)

That if we pay little heed to ourselves during our life, we will have little help at death

Everything in the world passes so swiftly that we see ourselves deprived of the advantages of fortune even before we realize we have received them. Yet despite this, we become neither better nor more detached, nor more eager for the eternal goods that alone deserve a place in the hearts of those who are religious and faithful. At the end of our life's course, we find it to be so empty of that with which it should be filled that all that remains to us in that moment is the sorrow of seeing ourselves without works, without worth, and, as a result, without hope.

---

[178] See n. 48 above. The reference is to Matt 11:12: the kingdom of heaven is carried off by violence.

[179] In seventeenth-century French, *piété*/piety may mean no more than a proper respect for anything to do with the church or the Christian religion, or it may mean an indefinable mixture of dutiful reverence, dedicated faithfulness, godliness, and what today we would call spirituality.

CLXXXV (185)

On useless regrets at death

Just as there is a time when the consideration of our miseries is useful[180] for us, there is also a time[181] when, far from being useful, it serves only to plunge us into bitterness and affliction. As it is written: *Desiderium peccatorum peribit.*[182]

CLXXXVI (186)

On making good use of our life

It does not matter whether our life be long, but it must be holy.

CLXXXVII (187)

On abandoning God

Although it is not impossible to find God again after we have neglected him, it must be said that there is nothing more rare. Once God has spoken and knocked on the doors of our heart to no effect, he says nothing more and maintains a perpetual silence: *Haec fecisti et tacui.*[183]

---

[180] Reading *utile* "useful" with M for *inutile* "useless" in P, which is obviously incorrect and makes no sense. The point of this *Pensée* is that if we are to examine what we have done wrong, then we should do so while we are still alive so that something can be done about it. If we leave it to the point of death, all we will be left with will be bitter and useless regrets.

[181] I.e., at death.

[182] Ps 111:10: "The desire of sinners shall perish." This last sentence, with its Latin quotation, is omitted in P. The same thing occurs in *Pensées* 187 and 240. It seems that the editor of the *Pensées*, unlike Marsollier, did not expect his readers to understand Latin.

[183] Ps 49:21: "You have done these things and I was silent." The brief Latin quotation is omitted in P: see n. 182 above.

CLXXXVIII (188)

On the danger of delaying our changing our way of life[184]

No one has ever regretted losing no time in giving themselves to God. But there are an infinite number of people who, because they have delayed this, will pour forth tears for all eternity, and for these they will receive neither relief nor consolation.

CLXXXIX (189)

That in the world we need to act with propriety

We must so regulate the way we act with others that we do nothing to rebuff them or scare them away. We need to please in order to persuade, not by groveling compliance or by compromises that conflict with what we owe to truth, but in ways that engage and attract. When we enjoy someone's company, we are more inclined to believe what they say and let ourselves be persuaded.[185]

CXC (190)

On consolation in afflictions

Privations are hard and grievous when they meet with resistance from the heart, but whatever their nature may be, when we trace them back to their source and see them for what they really are in a spirit of submission,[186] they are truly good for us. Even in this world we obtain from God the reward for making good use of them while we await the crown he is preparing for us in the next.

---

[184] See also *Pensées* 7, 82, and 148.

[185] M¹: *à se persuader*; M² and P: *à se laisser persuader*.

[186] *Dépendance*, "dependence, submission, subjection, subordination."

CXCI (191)

Of the benefits to be found in [the attacks of] our enemies

It is a great adornment to appear at the Judgment of God weighed down by all the affronts and marks of ill will from men and women when we have endured them in peace, with patience, and, we say, with charity.

CXCII (192)

That unexpected[187] *ways [to God] are suspect*

There is no other way but that which Jesus Christ has set out for us by his word and his example. There is no other perfection that a Christian should know on earth save that of loving him and following him.

CXCIII (193)

That renunciation must be total

We very often see that those who have renounced businesses and fortunes that people regard as important entangle themselves all over again with petty trifles, which makes their first steps useless. After having snapped cables and broken iron chains, they are now held back by hairs and spiders' threads! The destiny of Christians is nothing less than to possess the whole of eternity, a kingdom of blessing and glory. Do you not see that the stupidest thing of all is to deprive oneself willingly of this by the pleasure one takes in building houses of mud and straw?

---

[187] The French expression is *vies extraordinaires*, ways that are out of the ordinary, unusual, unfamiliar, unexpected, singular, not what they should be, weird. We may compare *Pensée* 223.

CXCIV (194)

On falling [into sin] in the monastery[188]

Even though [monastic] solitudes are shelters and havens, there are still times when it is possible to come to shipwreck there as in the midst of the sea.

CXCV (195)

On judging our neighbor favorably

All the ways of men and women are so convoluted and mysterious that God alone knows them perfectly. What charity wants is that when we do not know a person's intentions, and do not fully understand the motives for what they do, we should judge them favorably.

CXCVI (196)

That apart from God there is only confusion

Our paths are straight only insofar as we have God before our eyes. If ever we part company with him, there is nothing in us but disorder and confusion.

CXCVII (197)

That in all places God acts on behalf of his elect

The mercy of God knows no limits, and in all places as in all circumstances his omnipotent hand protects and sustains those who have the happiness to belong to him.

---

[188] Lit. "in the solitude," but here *la solitude* can only mean a monastery.

CXCVIII (198)

On distrusting the way people judge us

We should not believe what people say of us, whether it be good or bad. People often ascribe to us wickedness we do not actually possess. As for the good, there is so little of it that whatever is said of it is always an exaggeration.

CXCIX (199)

That without the love of God, withdrawal [from the world] is useless

Withdrawal [from the world] is useless if it does not purify us from every impression of worldly things. There is no point in fleeing human society if we do not come closer to God. To reap a real profit from the advantage we have in being separated from others, we must be wholly united with him for the love of whom we separate ourselves from them.

CC (200)

On the dangers of the world

There is no purity that is not tarnished by interaction with the world, for it conceals a secret and contagious malice from which it is almost impossible to defend oneself. Those who see this with more holiness are not entirely protected from it, but they receive the very slightest wounds. But whether it be much or little, [any interaction with the world] must either taint or corrupt.

CCI (201)

On the sweetness of withdrawal [from the world]

When one loves and enjoys withdrawal and solitude, and has found one's pleasure and consolation in God alone, there is great cost in descending and coming to a stop on earth. [The earth] is only for those who bind themselves to it and who follow its inclinations and maxims. Their thoughts, like their hearts, are wholly earthly.

CCII (202)

On the usefulness of withdrawal [from the world]

The effects of a long period of withdrawal are normally inward peace and feelings of consolation, a reward for the faithfulness of those who have persevered for some time in the service of God. It is true that we leave the world, but the world does not stop following those who leave it, and the habits we have contracted there are destroyed only as a result of watching over all that we do with the greatest care.

CCIII (203)

That we need [189] *to flee from the world to be united* [190] *with God*

The great secret to being aware of God, to winning his presence, and to making sure that it does not escape us when it has become familiar to us, is to love neither the world nor anything that the world contains,[191] except for what pertains to God and to the love of God. All those things to which, for their own sake, we give place in our heart are seeds of those aberrations and [spiritual] aridity that cause us so much pain. To possess God by using both our spirit and our heart[192] is something so wonderful that we must do all that we can to obtain that grace.

---

[189] P omits *nécessaire*.

[190] There are three verbs in this *Pensée* that look as if they might have mystical meaning, but do not. They are *unir*, *sentir*, and *posséder*, "to unite, to sense, and to possess." But for Rancé, to unite with God is to do his will, to sense God simply means to be aware of him or to feel his presence, and to possess him is to rejoice in feeling him present. At no time are we talking about the rapturous unity of spirit, *unitas spiritus*, that we find in (for example) William of Saint-Thierry. This is a matter we discussed at some length in chap. 2 of this book.

[191] M¹: *qu'il enferme*; M² and P: *qu'il renferme*. The two verbs mean the same thing.

[192] See n. 167 above. Here *esprit* and *cœur* might be translated "head and heart."

CCIV (204)

On neglecting eternal things

What can possibly be more astonishing than to see people doing everything in their power for the sake of their health, and doing so little for their salvation? They take almost infinite care to preserve their body and make not the slightest effort to sanctify their soul. We call this living according to the senses, not according to the spirit,[193] and preferring time that is nothing to eternity that is everything.

CCV (205)

That it is useful to distrust ourselves

Distrusting ourselves is useful when it does not produce anxiety, discouragement, or confusion, but rather turns us towards God and leads us to seek in his protection what we can never find in our own weakness. We will never be let down when we hope more for his mercy and have less reason to hope for his justice.

CCVI (206)

That we should sacrifice our reputation to God

Our reputation should be in the hands of God. If it is useful for his glory, he will preserve it; if it serves no purpose in this, there is little point in concerning ourselves about it. It should be enough for us to be vindicated at the judgment of God and in the testimony of our own conscience. Truly, all that we are is what we are in the eyes of God; and what we are[194] can be neither increased nor lessened by human opinion.

---

[193] In this case, the spirit/*esprit* is the whole inner being of a person.

[194] *Notre vertu*: *vertu* here is not so much virtue as our quality, condition, value, or what we are. It is virtue in the sense that some plants have a healing virtue.

CCVII (207)

On the dangers of learning[195]

Erudition is the reef on which humility founders, and vanity, which is the most common result of study, has often inflicted a thousand mortal wounds on the hearts of scholars who, despite all their enlightenment, were not even aware of what was going wrong.

CCVIII (208)

That God is jealous for those who belong to him

It takes very little to remove God from souls he has chosen and destined to apply themselves entirely to him. As he himself says,[196] he looks on them with jealousy, and he will not tolerate the slightest falling away[197] or the least reservation.

CCIX (209)

That bad intentions spoil our best actions

We are usually led to good by human motives. Sometimes our intentions are pure, but they get mixed up with incidents and circumstances that are not. We examine ourselves; we find what we seek—and what we find deserves punishment rather

---

[195] See chap. 1, n. 27. Much could be written on this (and has been), and a full discussion would take us deep into the controversy between Rancé and Dom Jean Mabillon on the question of monastic studies. See Bell, *Understanding Rancé*, 111–14, 315–20, and the index, 365, s.v. "Monastic studies, controversy over." To this may now be added David N. Bell, "Armand-Jean de Rancé on Reading: What, Why, and How?" *Cistercian Studies Quarterly* 50 (2015): 161–93.

[196] See Exod 20:5; 34:14; Deut 4:23-24; 5:9; 6:15; and especially Josh 24:19: *And Joshua said to the people: "You will not be able to serve the Lord, for he is a holy God, and mighty and jealous, and will not forgive your wickedness and sins."*

[197] *Le moindre partage* "the least sharing." To share God with something or someone is a form of idolatry, and idolatry (as Saint Paul makes clear) is a very grievous sin.

than meriting any reward. And it often happens that God is angered by what satisfies men and women.

CCX (210)

On the advantage of being uncertain about the hour of our death

We are blessed that our destinies are in the hands of God. When it comes to the limits that he wishes to set to our life, we must will only his will, and submit ourselves in perfect resignation to every one of his commands.

CCXI (211)

That charity does not demand trust

Although we set no limits to the charity we should have for our enemies, we can put our trust in it.[198]

CCXII (212)

On willing only what God wills

The only happiness in this world is simply to be what God wants us to be. We often boast that this is so when it is not the case, and claim to have laid down the burdens that overwhelm us with a view to thinking ourselves more free and [able to] follow his paths more easily. Yet he leaves these things to us, because it is more useful for us to deal with them.

---

[198] This is a very odd saying that appears in identical form in both M and P. The French is straightforward (*Quoique nous me mettions aucune borne a la charité que nous devons avoir pour nos enemis, nous en pouvons mettre à notre confiance*); the meaning is not. The text seems to imply that although it is our duty to have limitless charity for our enemies, our human frailty will render this impossible—but whatever charity we do have, that we may trust. Yet the subtitle tells us that charity does not demand trust (*la charité ne nous oblige pas à la confiance*). I am not at all sure what Rancé is saying here.

CCXIII (213)

On being faithful to God

God remains ever the same for those who serve him, and once he has given himself to us,[199] it is our faithfulness that keeps him there and holds him. Only our ingratitude leads him to withdraw.[200]

CCXIV (214)

On the changeability of the world and the stability of our trust in God

The world may amuse us, but anything we can hope from it passes like a flash of lightning. Only in the protection of God is to be found unchanging stability, and that alone can protect us from the deadly effects that the things of this life, both good and bad, have on our hearts. If we are to live and die happily, we must place ourselves entirely in the hands of God.[201]

CCXV (215)

That God alone can quieten the restlessness[202] of the human heart

The more we reduce our spirit to a true simplicity, the more God will be its master. We get anxious and perturbed about how to belong to God, and it often happens that instead of following his word, which would provide us with every consolation, we follow our own imagination, we lose our way, and all we find is confusion and agitation.

---

[199] M omits "to us."

[200] Further on the sin of ingratitude, see *Pensée* 126 and n. 98 and n. 132.

[201] Lit. "We must be in *un abandonnement entier*": see n. 103 above.

[202] M: *l'inquiétude*; P: *l'incertitude*.

CCXVI (216)

On the reasons for belated conversions

It is very common to form a desire for conversion with no effect whatever. We fall into this misfortune when we put off responding to the voice that speaks to us. A holy life is the only preparation that can assure us of a holy death.[203]

CCXVII (217)

On the usefulness of a good example

Example is the best possible means we can use to lead others to virtue. When God has become known to us, it would be a great misfortune to hide it from others by what we ourselves do.

CCXVIII (218)

On how our duties should be regulated

We must measure ourselves in everything by the graces God has given us and by what he asks of us.

CCXIX (219)

On real and spurious virtues

Those who belong to God conceal the real virtues they have received and make sure that they are not seen. Those who belong to the world consider [these virtues] to be spurious and show that they do not possess them.

CCXX (220)

On the usefulness of afflictions

Afflictions are the portion of those souls who belong to Jesus Christ. Just as there is nothing that raises them higher in the sight of God, there is also nothing he procures for them in greater quantity.

---

[203] Se also *Pensée* 136 and n. 73 above.

CCXXI (221)

On allying oneself with grace

The same graces that save some condemn others.[204] We must therefore use our utmost diligence to profit from the gifts of God and to make the most of the talents[205] we have received[206] from his mercy.

CCXXII (222)

On God's goodness to those who serve him

God upholds the souls that serve him. When he allows them to be tempted, he never fails to alleviate their bitterness by secret arrangements that are the pure effects of his mercy. We cannot go wrong if we place ourselves entirely in his hands.[207] He knows how to mix good things with bad and has us find what is best for us in the former as in the latter.

CCXXIII (223)

On the only way to heaven

It is the height of audacity to claim that we can enter the kingdom of God by any other ways than those by which he has led his saints there.[208]

CCXXIV (224)

On the value of trusting in God

We must place our salvation[209] in the hands of God in the assured belief that nothing is more precious to him than the sanctification of his Elect, and that nothing compels him more to take care to save them than the trust they put in him.

---

[204] We may compare *Pensée* 125.
[205] See Matt 25:14-30; Luke 19:12-27.
[206] M: *nous recevons* (present); P: *nous avons reçu* (perfect).
[207] *Quand on s'abandonne*: see n. 103 above.
[208] We may compare *Pensée* 192.
[209] M: *sort* "destiny"; P: *salut* "salvation."

CCXXV (225)

On the misfortune of a negligent soul

It is a great misfortune to have God regret the marks he has given us of his mercies by neglecting to make use of them and [neglecting] to respond to them by being faithful in our lives.

CCXXVI (226)

On the dangers of dealings with the world

Any interaction and any dealings we retain with the world are a cause of grave dissipation [of our spiritual resources].[210] When the heart receives such damaging blows and impressions, it is virtually impossible for it not to fall into apathy and for that piety[211] not to be perverted. We fill ourselves up with people and things with whom we have dealings, but the more the world plays a part in what we do and think, the less we give to God.

CCXXVII (227)

On belonging to God completely[212]

All Christians have an indispensable obligation to belong to God and to avoid at all costs anything that may displease him. But this duty must be regulated in proportion to the graces we have received from his divine goodness. He is not satisfied with what we feel in our hearts: he wants action! [And his will is] that there should be nothing in our whole life that is not ordered by him and according to his intentions.

---

[210] *Dissipation* does not mean here dissipation in the sense of debauchery, decadence, or dissolute living, but squandering, dispersing, or wasting. It is effectively a technical term of seventeenth-century French spirituality.

[211] See n. 179 above.

[212] *Sans partage* "without division, without sharing, undivided": see n. 197 above.

CCXXVIII (228)

That there should be no holding back with regard to [the things that pertain to] God

God has no wish that souls whom he has touched with his fear and whom, by his mercy, he has snatched back from the ways of death[213] should have any reservations when it comes to him. [He has no wish] that they should let themselves be besmirched by interaction with the world and its affairs, for these inspire only principles and affections wholly contrary to those he demands of people who have the joy of serving him.

CCXXIX (229)

That taking sides [in ecclesiastical conflicts] is dangerous

It is dangerous to take sides in the conflicts that spring up in the Church. In such encounters we easily become impassioned and lose our temper. We conceal ourselves from ourselves. We cloak what we do under the pretext of a love of truth, and resentment is often regarded as holy ardor. And what happens? Truth, which once held pride of place in our sight, degenerates into injustice, and charity is changed into feelings of contempt or hatred for those who hold a different opinion. We owe much to truth. We owe no less to charity. Can we defend one without the other?

CCXXX (230)

That we ourselves should never interfere in the works of God

It often happens that God's plans are ruined and show anything but the success one hopes for because we ourselves interfere in what is going on and mix ourselves up in it without any direction. God has often averted his eyes from his works

---

[213] See Prov 14:12 and 16:25.

because of the unworthiness of the hands that have been put to work there.[214]

CCXXXI (231)

On the cure for discouragement

We are protected from every temptation of discouragement and distrust if everything we do has as its basis a complete confidence in the goodness of God, and if we take our stand on the assurance that he himself has given that those who hope in him will never be confounded.[215]

CCXXXII (232)

On the cure for tedium[216] *in the [monastic] solitude*

Nothing is more effective in protecting us from the tedium that so often troubles us in our withdrawal [from the world] than the thought that we are waiting for Jesus Christ, that his return to this world cannot be delayed, and that there is no moment in which he cannot surprise us. For when he rends the clouds and comes, surrounded by fire and flame, to judge mortals,[217] the only ones who shall look on this with consolation are those who have lived their lives in the expectation and belief in his coming.

---

[214] The basis of this *Pensée* is submission to the will of God, something we have heard so many times before. Our business is to cooperate willingly with God's will in bringing his works to fruition. If, however, we introduce our own self-will into the process in an effort to "improve" on the will of God— if we meddle or interfere in his business (the French verb is *s'ingérer*)—the results will be disastrous and God's plans will be ruined.

[215] See Ps 24:3; Rom 10:11. See also n. 228 below.

[216] *Ennui*: see n. 10 above.

[217] M: *les morts* "the dead"; P: *les mortels* "mortals."

CCXXXIII (233)

On the danger of setting a bad example

We must be careful to avoid any company that can distance us from God. There is nothing to be feared more than a bad example, for often enough we do things to oblige people that we would not do by inclination.

CCXXXIV (234)

On the reason for almsgiving

There is nothing more highly commended in Scripture than taking care of the poor.[218] They are the members of Jesus Christ, and what we do for them, we do for him.[219] If we are conscious of our own needs, we will be much more disposed to tend to those of others.

CCXXXV (235)

On excusing our neighbors' failings

God's goodness in excusing our own failings ought to lead us to bear with those of others. It is far safer to excuse wickedness where it exists than to condemn it[220] where it does not.

CCXXXVI (236)

On moderation in expressing our opinions

We never express our opinions with too much vehemence and enthusiasm. It is better to be prudent and yield than to prevail at the expense of charity.

---

[218] See, for example, Matt 5:3; Mark 10:21; Luke 4:18; 6:20; Gal 2:10; and many other places.

[219] See Matt 25:31-46.

[220] M adds *souvent* "often," but the reading in P is better.

CCXXXVII (237)

An excellent moral principle

The proprieties demanded by our position in life never excuse us from the laws of Christianity. We may enjoy them, but we must never become attached to them. A law that comes from a lesser authority must always yield to a law that comes from a greater authority.

CCXXXVIII (238)

On indifference to worldly goods

Whatever dignities, goods, and honors may come to us, we receive them all as if they come from the hand of God. We never anticipate them by our own wishes, and we are always ready to experience their loss with resignation and peace.

CCXXXIX (239)

That we must fight against injustice

We are allowed—and, indeed, sometimes required—to fight against human injustice. But it must be done in such a way that it is clear that it is not a result of passion or emotion,[221] but that justice alone makes us act in this way.

CCXL (240)

On using our authority

The weight of our authority should never serve to overwhelm anyone. It is given to us by God to do good, never to do evil. *Sic praesis ut prosis*, says Saint Bernard.[222]

---

[221] "passion or emotion" = *la passion*.

[222] Bernard, *De consideratione*, III.i.2; SBOp 3:432: "Lead in order to serve." "Lead," Bernard continues (echoing Matt 24:45), "so as to be a faithful and prudent servant whom the Lord has set up over his family." P, as usual, omits the Latin: see nn. 182 and 183 above. Apart from his references to Jesus Christ, this is the only time in the *Pensées* when Rancé quotes an authority.

CCXLI (241)

That friendship must take second place to justice

We owe to our parents and our friends a respect and decorum that everyone should recognize. But our desire to accommodate them should never lead us to do anything unjust. What we owe to God must prevail in everything.

CCXLII (242)

On how we should behave with respect to our servants [223]

How we look after our household is of first importance. The servants owe us service. We owe them a good example, proper attention to all they do, and a positive attitude that may lessen the yoke of their servitude.[224] How is it that they are not in our place? Why are they not our masters? This is what we must sometimes ask ourselves.[225]

---

[223] Having servants, *les domestiques*, is somewhat rare nowadays, but in Rancé's France they were an integral and vital part of society. The more aristocratic the family, the greater the number of servants. There were those, therefore, who solicited Rancé's advice as to how they should deal with their *domestiques*. One such was Élisabeth Marguerite d'Orléans, a first cousin of Louis XIV, who was born on 26 December 1646. On 15 May 1667 she married Louis-Joseph de Lorraine, duke of Guise and duke of Angoulême, titular head of the House of Guise. She then became Madame de Guise, and, in France, she was known by this title until her death in 1696. She was a proud and haughty dame, very conscious of her elevated position in society, and she governed a large household. Rancé became her spiritual director and, in 1697, published his *Conduite chrétienne adressée à Son Altesse Royalle Madame de Guise*. Chap. 17 of the book—pages 155 to 161—is devoted to "Règlement des Domestiques & des principaux Officiers de la maison." See further David N. Bell, " 'A Holy Familiarity': Prayer and Praying According to Armand-Jean de Rancé," *Cistercian Studies Quarterly* 51 (2016): 355–58, 369.

[224] See Gal 5:1.

[225] The *Pensées et réflexions* were published in 1767. Just over twenty years later came the French Revolution.

CCXLIII (243)

On the usefulness of sufferings

The cross is essential for Christians: to live as a Christian is to live in suffering. There is nothing that can corrupt the heart more easily than living too long in too great prosperity. There is nothing more instructive than adversity.

CCXLIV (244)

On the rule[226] *[that prevents us] from being deluded*

Prudence is the guiding principle of piety and all good intentions. God's charity is wholly filled with wisdom. Anything that is not in accordance with these rules, however good it may appear, is not in fact good. This is the rule that protects us against delusions.

CCXLV (245)

On following God's plans

An ordinary life is not enough for those whom God has withdrawn from the world only so that they might have the means of leading an extraordinary one. How happy are they to be nothing in the world and to turn all their hopes towards eternity!

CCXLVI (246)

On why we should trust [in God]

What should establish our trust is that God's goodness is infinite, while our infidelities, however great and numerous they may be, have limits.

---

[226] The rule/*règle* is the rule of guiding all that we do by a combination of prudence and charity. By judging what we do in this way, we will not be deluded or led astray.

CCXLVII (247)

On the benefits of humility

It is not enough to humble[227] oneself in the eyes of God: we must also do so before men and women. God yields to humble souls, and he never resists a contrite and humbled heart.[228]

CCXLVIII (248)

On putting all our hope in God

To set limits on our hopes is to offer insult to God, for he sets no limits on the love he has for us. The more we think ourselves unworthy of being heard by God, the more we should press him to alleviate our great misery.

CCXLIX (249)

On the usefulness of inward sufferings

In whatever inward suffering we find ourselves, we must wait on God in silence and peace. The lack of response[229] that he sometimes allows us to experience has[230] its uses and purposes. Our steadfast faith and our fidelity to our duties touch the heart of God and have great power in soliciting his mercy.

CCL (250)

On how to please God

As much as sin will be the object of our heart's hatred, so our heart will be the object of God's love.

---

[227] See n. 38 above. "To humble oneself" is better here.

[228] Ps 50:19: *Cor contritum et humiliatum, Deus, non dispicies*, "A contrite and humbled heart, O God, you will not despise."

[229] *L'insensibilité*: the apparent indifference shown by God when we pray to him and nothing happens. That nothing happens, says Rancé, is itself a happening.

[230] Reading *a* with M² and P, not *à* with M¹, which is obviously a typographical error.

CCLI (251)

On what we owe to truth

We must not love ourselves more than truth, and we should not be afraid to lay ourselves open when it is a question of maintaining the truth and defending it.

CCLII (252)

On the merit of charity

Charity gives worth to what we do, and we please God to the degree that we love him.

CCLIII (253)

That simplicity is the source of tranquility

Simplicity gives us peace and tranquility. Without it there is only agitation and disquiet. This simplicity consists in cutting ourselves off from everything useless and being satisfied with what alone is needful.[231]

CCLIV (254)

That the heart is not made for created things

Human happiness is not to be found in created things: we seek something that is not of this world. This idea, given us by God, gives birth to love, and love to desire. But all too often this desire produces only sighs of longing. And it seems that however high our heart rises towards this goal, the goal rises yet higher and retreats even further from our heart!

---

[231] There may be an echo here of Luke 10:41-42: Martha is troubled about many things, *porro unum est necessarium*, "but one thing alone is needful." Such is the part chosen by Mary.

CCLV (255)

On the grave danger of the world

It is not the same with created things.[232] They follow us everywhere. They continually present themselves before our eyes, and through our eyes they enter our spirit. [Once there] they divide it,[233] and bring with them disquiet and dissipation.[234]

CCLVI (256)

On the danger of conversations

Words and conversations, however well regulated and innocent they may be, never fail to leave us with unfortunate impressions and produce confused ideas that are very difficult to rectify. They open doors in us as if to lead us out of ourselves. They fill us with fancies and empty daydreams that are the ill-omened sources of that almost infinite number of distractions and deficiencies we experience in our prayer and other exercises of piety. To truly belong to God, we must seek solitude.

CCLVII (257)

That God's will is the true food of the soul

Jesus Christ says that his food is to do the will of his Father.[235] Our emptiness and aridity come from our not feeding on this food. This food never fails us, since we can never avoid doing the will of God. But it is not enough just to do his will: we must also wish to do it. Despite themselves, the demons do his will, but they certainly do not want to.

---

[232] We are here following on logically from the end of the previous *Pensée*. There we are told that happiness is not to be found in created things; here we are told why. We may compare *Pensée* 202: "It is true that we leave the world, but the world does not stop following those who leave it."

[233] *Elles le partagent*: see nn. 197 and 212.

[234] *La dissipation*: see n. 210.

[235] John 4:34.

CCLVIII (258)

That sinners may be compared to demons[236]

Everything obeys God naturally. The whole of nature is obliged to carry out his orders, and it is this that gives movement to all beings. Demons and sinners are the only ones who obey him despite themselves.

CCLIX (259)

On living while awaiting [the coming of] Jesus Christ

We ought to live in this world as the Holy Fathers lived in limbo:[237] that is, to live in faith, in the expectation, and with holy zeal for the coming of Jesus Christ.

The End of the *Pensées* of the Abbot of la Trappe.[238]

---

[236] This *Pensée* continues the theme of the previous one.

[237] *les limbes* = the *limbus patrum,* "limbo of the Fathers," i.e., that state of being in which the saints of the Old Testament were thought to be confined until they were set free by Christ in the *descensus ad inferos,* the "descent into hell," mentioned in the Apostles' Creed.

[238] Such is the ending in M¹ and P (M¹ has *l'Abbé;* P has *M[onsieur]. l'Abbé*). M² simply has *Fin* "End."

Selected Bibliography

Bell, David N. "Bread of Angels: Armand-Jean de Rancé on the Eucharist with a Translation of his Conference for the Feast of Corpus Christi." *Cistercian Studies Quarterly* 52 (2017): 277–309.

Bell, David N. "Daniel de Larroque, Armand-Jean de Rancé, and the Head of Madame de Montbazon." *Cîteaux – Commentarii cistercienses* 53 (2002): 305–31.

Bell, David N. *The Image and Likeness: The Augustinian Spirituality of William of Saint-Thierry.* Cistercian Studies series 78. Kalamazoo, MI: Cistercian Publications, 1984.

Bell, David N. *A Saint in the Sun: Praising Saint Bernard in the France of Louis XIV.* Cistercian Studies series 271. Collegeville, MN: Cistercian Publications, 2017.

Bell, David N. *Understanding Rancé: The Spirituality of the Abbot of La Trappe in Context.* Cistercian Studies series 205. Kalamazoo, MI: Cistercian Publications, 2005.

Butler, Charles. *The Lives of Dom Armand-Jean Le Bouthillier de Rancé, Abbot Regular and Reformer of the Monastery of La Trappe; and of Thomas à Kempis, the Reputed Author of "The Imitation of Christ." With Some Account of the Principal Religious and Military Orders of the Roman Catholic Church.* London: Luke Hansard & Sons, 1814.

Charencey, Charles-Félix-Hyacinthe, comte de. *Histoire de l'abbaye de la Grande-Trappe.* Mortagne: Georges Meaux, 1896–1911.

Christian Spirituality: Origins to the Twelfth Century. Vol. 1 of 3. Ed. Bernard McGinn, John Meyendorff, and Jean Leclercq. New York: Herder and Herder, 1985.

A Dictionary of Christian Spirituality. Ed. Gordon S. Wakefield. London: SCM Press, 1983.

Exauvillez, Philippe-Irenée Boistel d'. *Histoire de l'abbé de Rancé, réformateur de la Trappe*. Paris: Debécourt, 1842.

A History of Religion in Britain: Practice and Belief from Pre-Roman Times to the Present. Ed. Sheridan Gilley and W. J. Sheils. Oxford: Wiley-Blackwell, 1994.

Kleinz, John P. *The Theory of Knowledge of Hugh of Saint Victor.* Washington, DC: Catholic University of America Press, 1944.

Krailsheimer, Alban J. *Armand-Jean de Rancé, Abbot of la Trappe: His Influence in the Cloister and the World*. Oxford: Oxford University Press, 1974.

Larroque, Daniel de. *Les Véritables motifs de la Conversion de l'abbé de la Trappe, avec quelques réflexions sur sa vie & sur ses écrits, ou Les Entretiens de Timocrate & de Philandre sur le livre qui a pour titre Les S. Devoirs de la Vie Monastique*. Cologne: Pierre Marteau, 1685.

Luddy, Ailbe J. *The Real de Rancé: Illustrious Penitent and Reformer of Notre Dame de la Trappe*. London and New York: Arthur M. Gilbert & Son, 1931.

Marsollier, Jacques. *La vie de Dom Armand-Jean de Bouthillier de Rancé, abbé régulier et réformateur du Monastère de la Trappe*. Paris: J. de Nully, 1703; Paris: Chez Savoy, 1758.

McManners, John. *Death and the Enlightenment: Changing Attitudes to Death among Christians and Unbelievers in Eighteenth-Century France*. London/New York: Oxford University Press, 1981.

Principe, Walter H. "Toward Defining Spirituality." *Studies in Religion/Sciences religieuses* 12 (1983): 127–41.

Rancé, Armand-Jean de. *Abbé de Rancé: Correspondance*. 4 vols. Ed. Alban J. Krailsheimer. Paris: Cerf, 1993.

Rancé, Armand-Jean de. *De la sainteté et des devoirs de la vie monastique*. Paris: F. Muguet, 1683.

Schneiders, Sandra M. "Spirituality in the Academy." *Theological Studies* 50 (1989): 676–97.

Solignac, Aimé. "Spiritualité." *Dictionnaire de spiritualité*. Paris: G. Beauchesne et ses fils, 1990.

The Spirituality of Western Christendom. Ed. E. Rozanne Elder. Cistercian Studies series 30. Kalamazoo, MI: Cistercian Publications, 1978.

The Study of Spirituality. Ed. Cheslyn Jones, Geoffrey Wainwright, and Edward Yarnold. Oxford: Oxford University Press, 1986.

Swanson, Robert N. *Catholic England: Faith, Religion and Observance Before the Reformation*. Manchester and New York: Manchester University Press, 1993.

Tinsley, Lucy. *The French Expressions for Spirituality and Devotion: A Semantic Study*. Washington, DC: Catholic University of America Press, 1953.

Vauchez, André. *The Spirituality of the Medieval West: The Eighth to the Twelfth Century*. Trans. Colette Friedlander. Cistercian Studies series 145. Kalamazoo, MI: Cistercian Publications, 1993.

Index to the *Pensées*

The numbers refer to the numbering of the *Pensées*.

Index to Part One

Entries are cited by page number.